EURIPIDES
MEDEA · HIPPOLYTUS
THE BACCHAE

EURIPIDES (c. 477–405 b.c.)

EURIPIDES

MEDEA
HIPPOLYTUS
THE BACCHAE

Newly translated by
PHILIP VELLACOTT

Illustrated by
MICHAEL AYRTON

The 100 Greatest Books Ever Written

Collector's Edition
Bound in Genuine Leather

$\frac{\varepsilon}{\wp}$

The Easton Press
NORWALK, CONNECTICUT

The three tragedies in this volume were produced, respectively, in 431, 428, and 406 B.C. They are among the ten dramas included in the earliest extant Euripides manuscripts, compiled about the fourth century A.D.; another early ms. collection of eighteen dramas is believed to represent odd volumes from an edition edited by Aristophanes of Byzantium c. 200 B.C. The earliest printed editions containing these three plays in the original Greek are those of J. Lascaris (Florence, 1496) and M. Masurus (Aldus Manutius, Venice, 1503). Important translations into English include the prose versions by E. P. Coleridge (1891) and those in verse by A. S. Way (1894-98), Gilbert Murray (1902-06), Rex Warner (1961), and Philip Vellacott (published by Penguin Books, Ltd.; copyright © 1953, 1954, 1963 by Philip Vellacott).

PUBLISHER'S PREFACE

OF THE THREE greatest tragic dramatists of ancient times, Aeschylus (525–456 B.C.) is the representative of the newly evolved imperial city-state of Athens, Sophocles (496–406) of its prime, and Euripides (C. 477–405) of a period in which big-city ills and frustrations had become manifest. Euripides' popularity increased after his death as his plays survived into a Hellenic world that in significant ways was closer to our own time than to that of his contemporaries.

Euripides was born on the island of Salamis, which is just off the Greek mainland near Piraeus, the seaport of Athens. An oracle led his father to believe that Euripides would be a victor in athletic contests, whereupon he insisted on training the boy in wrestling and boxing. Euripides won some honors in local games, but must have realized that he was unsuited to that sort of life. He later looked down upon athletics as well as upon oracles. He tried painting, and then, at the age of eighteen, began writing tragedy. Euripides had found his career.

The dramatist saw his first productions performed at the religious festival of 454 B.C., when he was about twenty-three. The judges gave him third prize. At these festivals, which were held twice a year, the major feature was the presentation of plays written just for the celebration. Three playwrights were invited to submit a group of four plays each. A panel of judges awarded the prizes. With but three dramatists participating, the first prize was a particularly great honor.

Over the years, Aeschylus won thirteen firsts and Sophocles twenty-four, more than any other playwright. But after Euripides' death, *his* plays were reproduced and admired more than those of all his competitors. As a result, nineteen of Euripides' plays are extant, whereas we have only seven each by Aeschylus and Sophocles. Of these nineteen tragedies we have selected for the present

i

▣▣

volume the three that are considered to be his most important and exciting. In the chronological order of their presentation in the theater on the southeast side of the Acropolis, they are:

Medea (431 B.C.), which won last prize yet quickly became one of the most popular Athenian dramas, and is probably the most famous Greek tragedy; *Hippolytus* (428), the only surviving play of those produced in the poet's lifetime known to have won a first prize; and *The Bacchae* (405), the swan song of Euripides, which won him a posthumous first prize and which remains one of his most provocative works.

The plays of Euripides dealt with the human dimensions of contemporary people; if they did not please the judges, they must have fascinated the audience. His failure to win the accolades of the Athenian critics did not prevent him from becoming a foremost literary figure in the Greek world. There is a story that some of the Athenians captured by their enemies in Sicily in 413 B.C. won their freedom by reciting a verse of Euripides to the admiring captors.

In 408 he left Athens to live at the court of Archelaus, king of Macedon, and died there in 405.

In his Introduction to this edition of Euripides, Philip Vellacott depicts the milieu in which the three tragedies were produced, and brilliantly analyzes their plots and characters. The translations, also made by Vellacott, are the most readable of all versions in English.

He comes by his skill after many years of study and teaching. Born in a little town in Essex, Philip Vellacott went to various schools, including St. Paul's, London. While there he gained a scholarship in classics to Magdalene College, Cambridge, where he won high honors. After teaching for twenty-five years at Dulwich College, London, where he produced a number of Shakespeare's plays, he retired to rural Wales.

Vellacott has translated all nineteen of Euripides' extant dramas, as well as the seven by Aeschylus. Many of his translations have been broadcast by the BBC, as has *An Island in Time*, one of the original plays he has written on Greek themes. He is also the author of a Latin course called *Ordinary Latin*, a book that has been called a revolutionary approach to the study of that language.

The illustrator of this edition is the renowned author, sculptor, and painter Michael Ayrton, who was born in London in 1921. He too had been educated at several schools before his parents gave up the idea of a formal Oxford education for Michael and sent him off to Vienna as an art student. He lived in Paris for two years until the outbreak of World War II, spent two years in the R. A. F., and was invalided out.

Ayrton's name became known when Sir John Gielgud commissioned him and fellow-artist John Minton to design the scenery and costumes for a production of *Macbeth*. This was followed by some designing for Sadler's Wells ballets and some sets for Covent Garden operas.

He has had a score of one-man shows of paintings, sculpture, and collages in England, on the Continent, and in the United States, and is represented in many museums in Britain, Canada, Israel, Australia, and this country. Ayrton's extensive travels have been mainly to Greece and Italy, where he became deeply interested in history and archaeology. Having been greatly influenced by the Greeks, he dwells on such themes as the Minotaur, the oracles, and especially his favorite myth, that of Daedalus and Icarus. He has produced paintings and sculpture on that subject, besides two books, *The Testament of Daedalus* and *The Maze Maker*, a novel. He has also published a book of essays, *Golden Sections*.

Of the numerous books adorned with illustrations by Michael Ayrton, the Euripides reflects most clearly his application of erudition to artistic skill and his instinct for dramatic composition.

Equally distinguished is the typographic designer responsible for the book's format. Will Carter of Cambridge is proprietor of The Rampant Lions Press, where (with the help of his partner and son, Sebastian) he continues to produce work of distinction. His accomplishments include the designing of two typefaces for the Monotype Corporation.

Will Carter is also a stonecutter and woodcutter. His wooden direction-markers at Cambridge University are so neatly and deftly done that tourists take pictures of them. He has lectured on type and typography in New York, San Francisco, and other American centers.

Suiting the amplitude and dignity of the text and the illustrations is the Walbaum type that Carter selected for the Euripides tragedies. It is the Monotype version of an eighteenth-century face. Walbaum, a German punchcutter, broke away from the black-letter types prevalent in his country. His letter-forms, which reveal the classic French influence, are characterized by an agreeable slight squareness underlying the curves. The size of the Walbaum used here is the spacious fourteen-point, with three points of leading between the lines.

For the title of the book and each of the three plays, Will Carter relied on his own skill as a lettermaker; he drew them in shaded open-faced capitals that have a classic, carved look, and added a series of Greek borders.

The frontispiece, based on traditional likenesses of Euripides, is the work of Richard Eichman. An admirer of the great Dutch painters and of the French neo-classicists, Eichman prepares all his pigments from basic materials. He was born in 1940 in Union Bridge, Maryland, where he teaches art. At the Peabody Conservatory in Baltimore he graduated with the highest honors in his class. Eichman also studied at the Schuler School of Fine Arts in Baltimore.

The high-quality wove paper has been specially made for this edition in a cream-white tone. The exclusive cover design, in classical style, is elegantly impressed on the genuine leather binding, and complemented by the gilding with which the page edges are decorated and protected. Other rare features shared by all volumes in this collection of *The 100 Greatest Books Ever Written* are the raised hubs of the backbone, the ribbon marker, and the moiré endleaves.

THE EASTON PRESS

ILLUSTRATIONS

CONTENTS

INTRODUCTION

HERE ARE THREE plays written in Athens in the second half of the fifth century B.C., intended for a single performance before an audience of thousands, both men and women, at a national religious festival. The stories of these plays all involve passion, error, misery, and death. They were the product of a very small but highly organized community of people who have perhaps never been equalled for their combination of vitality, wit, revenge-fulness, courage, cruelty, curiosity, intelligence, instinctive taste, devotion to beauty and clear thinking, and creative zest for every human enterprise. The joy which they found in all the ordinary occupations of life expressed itself in dancing and music on every possible occasion, in story-telling, especially the endless Homeric verse-sagas, in athletics, in magnificent public buildings, in contentment with the severe minimum of personal luxury, in the enjoyment of ships and horses, in making or using embroidered cloth, engraved metal, superb plates, cups, pots, and dishes all decorated with exquisite drawings or paintings, in the uninhibited pursuit and celebration of love in all its forms; and perhaps supremely in the two annual dramatic festivals, where for several consecutive days they sat from dawn in an open-air theatre watching tragedies of passion, error, misery, and death.

The poets who wrote these dramas were national figures; they were loved and hated, venerated and mocked; their plays were eagerly expected, critically listened to, avidly discussed; distrib-uted and read, learnt by heart, recited in private and public, and revived at later festivals and in theatres all over Greece for cen-turies after.

What did ancient Greeks find in these plays, that was of such value to them? When they left the theatre, few seem to have been depressed by what they had seen and heard. The great majority felt that human life had been shown in its true perspective; that the entire nature of the world had been clarified, its harshness and its beauty displayed in a pattern which they could accept with courage and without resentment; that from a tale of cruelty, despair, and death, strength could be gathered and truth learnt. If these seem insufficient enticements for a theatre audience in our own day, let us go further and outline the kind of truth the light-hearted, volatile Athenians got from their entertainment. The truth it offered was that virtue gives no security, but is still virtue; that justice is uncertain in its pursuit of crime, but is still justice; that the gods are always there, and it is dangerous to ignore them – but life is full of danger from other sources as well, and there are many crimes which rouse man's indignation but draw no reaction from gods; that prayers for deliverance will be unanswered as often as answered; that divine guidance in moral perplexity will be at best equivocal; that man's truest comfort comes from knowing he has only himself to rely on, with perhaps the help of a brother or friend. This kind of truth is unpalatable to modern man because only a small proportion of his life is really his own responsibility, the rest being looked after, for better or worse, by the vast machine of modern society. It was palatable to the Athenian because he looked after his life himself, and was also responsible for the lives of his fellow-citizens. The more one reads of these plays, the more one becomes aware of a coherent view of life that underlies them, one that avoids the errors both of modern religion and of modern irreligion; a faith centred primarily in man and in the inherent qualities – whatever their ultimate source may be – of the human race.

The view of life which I have outlined reached its full expression in the work of Euripides, whose first surviving tragedy, *Medea*, was produced in 431 B.C., at the beginning of the long war between Athens and Sparta. The first of the three Athenian dramatists, Aeschylus, who a little less than thirty years earlier was composing the *Oresteian Trilogy*, held a view that differed in one respect. He clung to a belief that the ruthlessness of natural processes and historical events could be somehow related to man's instinctive hunger for justice, and that Zeus, father of gods and men, though stern, was still concerned for man's ultimate welfare. The spiritual struggle for such a faith is vividly illustrated in the Choral Odes of *Agamemnon*. The second tragedian, Sophocles, did not argue about the gods; he was sure of their existence, of their holiness and justice, and of their cognizance of human affairs; baffling discrepancies between faith and fact were to him the natural result of man's confined vision and weak will. Euripides parted company with his two predecessors, and with the majority of his fellow-citizens; he did not abandon the religious view of life, but he re-directed it, and found the values which evoke reverence in spheres other than the moral sphere. The moral sphere, in his view, belongs exclusively to man.

Two lines of change led to the development of thought which we meet in these plays of Euripides. First, for several generations philosophers had been questioning every assumption, principle, and institution on which life in fifth-century Greece was based. The truth of legends, the validity of moral and social codes, the authority of the State, the existence of gods, the possibility of knowledge, the value of truth – all were questioned, defended, confuted, re-stated; free-thinkers were often regarded as a danger to their city, but in Athens at least they were given the right of free speech as long as the democracy lasted. In 407, three years before the end of the Peloponnesian war, Euripides at the age of seventy left Athens and accepted an invitation to live at the court of the king of Macedon; five years after the end of the war, Socrates was sentenced to death by an Athenian court for teaching young men to think for themselves on religious and moral questions. Democracy was over, and so was Attic tragedy; but philosophy was just beginning, based on the ferment of thought which had pre-occupied both Socrates and Euripides for a generation and more.

The other line of change which guided Euripides' ideas was the rapid growth of the Athenian 'empire'. After their victory over the

Persian fleet at Salamis in 480 B.C. the Athenians had soon assumed a leading position in the 'Confederacy of Delos', which had been organized to unify the defence of Greece against Persia. After some years the treasury of this Confederacy was transferred from Delos to Athens; and under the leadership of Pericles Athens exercised a tyrannical authority over the smaller cities and islands that were members, and used her power to flout justice in her own interest. In 510 B.C. Athens had expelled her own tyrant, Hippias, and established freedom as the basic principle of government; at Marathon and Salamis she had with superb courage defended Greek freedom against Persian tyranny; now she was herself becoming tyrant over half of the Greek world, and enriching her citizens and rebuilding the Acropolis at the expense of other cities.

The temptations to this course were powerful, the rewards of it, both to pride and to pocket, irresistible; the pursuit of it was still without excuse. Sophocles in his most famous play used the figure of Oedipus as an image of the 'tyrant city' (see *Oedipus at Thebes* by Bernard Knox); Euripides in the first play in this book gives us the utterly different figure of Jason, who is none the less a close-up portrait of contemporary Athenian arrogance. The change in national policy from unselfish heroism to unscrupulous greed had come about during the first forty years of Euripides' life. It taught him that the man who honoured goodness above the pursuit of power must not only look for no help from the gods, but be prepared also to find most men his enemies.

To set against this sombre outlook, Euripides offers two constant sources of comfort. First, if the gods disappoint us, that is our fault for misconceiving them. The nature of a god is not to be man's friend, nor man's enemy, nor man's moral guide. It is the Hebrew and Christian tradition that presents God as embodying what ought to be, the ideal; the Greek god is the opposite of this, and stands for *what is* – in human nature, in human society, and in the universe (see *The Twelve Olympians* by C. Seltman). Aphrodite, Artemis, Dionysus, are primal instincts in man's blood; Hera,

Apollo, Athene, Hermes, Hephaestus, and Ares represent arts and institutions in man's society; Zeus, Poseidon, and Demeter are powers of the cosmos outside and around him. The gods are the unchangeable facts of existence, the terms upon which man enters this world. Sun, wind, rain, the sea, fire, provide man with the necessities of life; they may also attack him, destroy his home, kill him. By prudence and courage, most men may bargain with the gods for a share of happiness; even the highest virtue cannot win security, nor does the criminal forfeit the beauty of the natural world. To recognize these facts, and to order one's life accordingly, is piety; to ignore or deny them is *hybris*, arrogance, the fundamental sin leading inevitably to disaster. The reason for worshipping these uncompromising gods is not simply fear; it is the love of their beauty, as is attested by the dancing and joyful festivity with which they were honoured by ordinary people all over Greece. And the beauty of the gods is not merely the visual or practical beauty so often sung of in the lyric Choruses of Euripides' plays – the loveliness of the sea and the sky, of fields of grain, of music, of a woman's body, of a craftsman's work, of a pact of friendship or a well-made law. Gods are beautiful because they are eternal and unchangeable, because their varying natures are balanced in a dignified cosmic harmony. With the gods, man knows where he is; their impervious objectivity gives him stability and therefore courage.

This leads directly to the second source of comfort offered by the view of life which Euripides presents in his plays. Because gods do not die, for them nothing is ever serious or urgent. The dying Hippolytus says to Artemis (and says it without resentment), 'Easy it is for you to sever our long fellowship'. Dying is never easy. It is the discipline of knowing his place in the world, his knowledge that death must come, that gives to man all his noblest qualities, love, pity, faithfulness, courage, the passion for justice. All these are inherent in man's mortality. Cadmus, in the last scene of *The Bacchae*, says despairingly to the god Dionysus, 'Have mercy on us; we have sinned. Your vengeance is too heavy; gods should not be like men, keeping anger for ever.' This theme recurs in play after play: morality, in the deepest human sense, is outside the sphere of gods. A moral relationship strong enough to deal with wrong that has been committed and suffered – this is something that only man can achieve; and man achieves it because he knows that both he and his enemy must die. We shall return to this subject in connexion with *Hippolytus*.

In *Medea*, the earliest extant tragedy of Euripides, the heroine is first shown as an oppressed victim claiming sympathy and longing for revenge. The opportunity comes, and the revenge exacted is so ferocious that the sympathy is forfeited. The same pattern appears also in *The Bacchae* and in a number of other plays of Euripides, notably *Hecabe* and *Ion*. The whole of Greek history during the poet's mature years was a series of revenges and counter-revenges growing ever more irresponsible and profitless, with the innocent always involved in the suffering of the guilty; and line after line in these plays castigates the self-defeating folly of war. The quality in Medea which would especially appeal to an Athenian audience is her overmastering desire for justice; but she shows that even this fundamental virtue, if not combined with the other fundamental virtue of control and proportion, leads to criminal and barbaric excess.

I said earlier that the Greek looked after his own life. This was true in many respects, but in one most vital of all: at the centre of the Greek way of life was the principle of reason and order, and this must at all costs be defended against barbarism. In spite of all the treachery, injustice, and self-seeking that poisoned Greek life in the fifth century, the Athenian still knew that his city embodied principles of culture and morality far superior to anything recognized in the Persian Empire. Order, proportion, respect for life and for individuality – these were publicly honoured in Greece, even if sometimes infringed; and their ultimate defence was each man's personal acceptance of the ideal, his vote in the Assembly, and his sword in the battle. Because only the purity of the race could maintain this principle, no Greek could have a non-Greek woman recognized as his legitimate wife. The urgency of this rule had not diminished in the seven or eight centuries which had passed since the time of Jason; his repellent arrogance was still relevant in Euripides' day. And just as in Jason a concern for civilized values is joined with a calculating coldness and an unscrupulous want of feeling, so in Medea warmth of feeling grows on the same stem as emotional excess and the propensity to violence. The lesson of this play – indeed of all these plays – is that civilized men ignore at their peril the world of instinct, emotion, and irrational experience. And the ending of *Medea* – with the Sun himself, the source of all life and warmth, vindicating the cause of passion, disorder, violent cruelty, against the cold, orderly, self-protective processes of civilized life – is a reminder that the universe is not on the side of civilization, and that a life combining order with happiness is something men must win for themselves in continual struggle with an unsympathetic environment.

Their devotion to justice drove thoughtful Athenians constantly to ask the question, When a wrong has been committed or a life taken, what is the proper way to deal with this affront to the universal sense of right? Aeschylus' answer in the *Oresteia* rejects the barbarous code of private revenge and substitutes the civilized method of passing sentence by majority vote in an established court. This is satisfactory to the legal mind, but does not help either the suffering of the victim or the conscience of the wrong-doer. The idea of forgiveness is not mentioned in the *Oresteia*. In Euripides this idea is mentioned a number of times as something that men pray to the gods for, and never get; or something that men can bestow on their fellow-men, but rarely do. *Hippolytus* is the one extant Greek tragedy in which we see a wrong committed by one man against another issuing in true repentance and forgiveness. That forgiveness is an important theme of the play is emphasized by several features. First, the prayer of the Old Slave in the opening scene, that Aphrodite will forgive the impious words of Hippolytus; then, the fact that Hippolytus is brutally unforgiving to Phaedra, and thus drives her

to the act which destroys him; lastly, the complete blindness to any
such idea shown by both Aphrodite and Artemis, who thus under-
line the truth that moral nobility belongs to man alone.

However, this theme of forgiveness occupies chiefly the last scene
of the play. The theme of the first half is, as in *Medea*, that 'Hell
hath no fury like a woman scorned'. At the beginning of the play, her
moral conscience is almost enough to make Phaedra end her life,
but not quite, for she weakens under the Nurse's pressure; and later
the cruelty of Hippolytus not only clinches her resolve, but stings
her pride to unscrupulous revenge. Euripides was regarded by his
contemporaries as a woman-hater, because he presented characters
such as Phaedra and Medea. In fact it was Athenian society, not
Euripides, that was guilty of misogyny. True, the life of Athenian
women contained in general much to enjoy; but in the eighty years
since the expulsion of the tyrant, Athenian men had experienced an
astonishing expansion of their political and mental horizon. It is
absurd to suppose that the generations which produced men of that
stamp did not produce women to match, but in that exhilarating
expansion women were given no active share at all. There must have
been many whom frustration and resentment drove to viciousness.
Euripides presents the case for women with truth and candour,
showing their unenviable position in a man-made society. 'Nothing
extenuate, nor set forth aught in malice' fairly describes his attitude
to Phaedra and to Medea, and to all his female characters. In his
extant work we find at least one ideal heroine, Polyxena in *Hecabe*;
there are a number of wholly bad men, but no wholly bad women.

Euripides wrote *The Bacchae* in Macedon, a year or two before
he died. It is more formal in style than most of his later plays. The
Chorus, which he had sometimes reduced almost to irrelevance,
here reverts to its earlier function as a participant in the drama. The
story is of the coming of the Dionysiac cult to Greece, an event
which can be given no certain date, though the ninth or eighth
century is a fair guess. This cult seems to have represented the
reaction of the free human spirit against the restrictions imposed by

civilization, by the growth of crowded cities, by the enforcement of laws, by the disciplines of war, and by the domination of man over woman. Its devotees saw in the life of animals a freedom and an innocence they themselves had lost. Under the stimulation of music and dancing they experienced a mass trance which gave them superhuman physical strength; they would pursue any wild animal within sight, and their fury reached its orgasm in the act of tearing the animal to pieces and eating its warm flesh. Bacchic groups of this kind were usually women, with a young man acting as their leader. The cult was at first regarded with natural suspicion, but soon Greek common-sense reached a compromise, and Dionysus was given a temple in Delphi next to Apollo's – the god of licence and the god of order symbolizing together the eternal Greek principle of proportion, 'nothing in excess'. There is little evidence to show whether Euripides had any reason for choosing Dionysus as a subject besides the god's tremendous dramatic potential; but it would not be surprising if the long strain of the war, with a state of actual siege recurring almost every summer for twenty-five years, had driven Athenians to seek emotional release in this kind of excitement.

The figure of Dionysus – he can hardly be called a 'character' – is different from that of other deities who appear in Euripides' plays. Aphrodite resents neglect, Apollo fails to answer prayers, Athene can be benevolent; but Dionysus has the dangerous aggressiveness of the newcomer. When he first appears, the battle is already joined, his victory already half won, his victim already shaken and weakened, though still showing confidence. Dionysus himself is 'the bull-horned god', and represents in his creative aspect the principle of all growing and self-renewing life; but in his more sinister aspect he represents *the beast in man* – an integral element of our human nature, which, if too much suppressed by 'civilization', calls to the restive human heart and evokes an eager and ecstatic response. The Bacchic ritual takes the form of a hunt, since hunting or being hunted is the natural occupation of wild animals. When the victim has been selected, in the course of the chase Dionysus himself enters into the victim's body, and thence into those who devour the victim, all alike 'possessed' by the god. For the main part of the action of the play Dionysus appears in the disguise of a young man who has led a group of Bacchic women from Lydia in Asia Minor through Thrace and into Greece; and his motive is the fact that his mother's family, the royal house of Thebes, have denied his divine birth, and his cousin, the puritan king Pentheus, has forbidden his worship in Thebes. Only in the final scene does Dionysus appear in his full glory as a god.

The Chorus represents visibly the whole female population of Thebes, who are said to have left their homes and to be out on the slopes of Mount Cithaeron in a state of trance. Their opening songs are full of gentleness and peace, with here and there an ominous word hinting at another side of their nature. They know that civilization is corrupt, cruel, and restrictive; they have cast off civilization and are therefore conscious of innocence, gentleness, and freedom. They are unaware of any civilized values which may have resisted corruption and promoted freedom and gentleness. Because there are unsound elements in conventional law, they call their own amorality 'soundness of mind'; because philosophy and learning sometimes neglect simple happiness, they call their own irresponsible innocence 'wisdom'; because cities are sometimes ugly and nations go to war, they claim that beauty and peace are only to be found in the wild life of the mountain-side. As the play proceeds, the other face of the Bacchic virtues is revealed: the imperviousness to pity or to reason, the unbridled urge to revenge, the readiness to jettison all those higher values which the slow progress of man has won to distinguish him from beasts. Each successive Choral Ode makes the theme of violence more explicit, while the theme of gentleness is used as though to allay fears roused by the increasing dominance of Dionysus in the action. Finally the Bacchae identify themselves with their partners away on the mountain, and in lines of terrifying force participate imaginatively in the dismemberment of Pentheus.

The crucial point in the character of Pentheus is that he is a

Dionysiac by nature. Violence is his answer to every problem, reason makes no appeal to him. Further, though he presents himself as the champion of law and order, the supposed disorderly behaviour of the Bacchae exerts on him an irresistible fascination; he is convinced that their religious dances are merely a pretext for drunkenness and sexual indulgence, and announces his intention to 'hunt' them from the mountain, to imprison them; even, later, to massacre them. His fear of what he himself is has made his whole character repressive; Cadmus, mourning over him, recalls that even Pentheus' kindness to his grandfather had found expression in threats against those who slighted the old man. The scene where Dionysus prepares his victim for sacrifice by dressing him in women's clothes shows Pentheus already removed from the world of reason and sanity into the mysterious amoral world (the world of 'black magic') which for animals, perhaps even for prehistoric man, blends beauty, cruelty, joy, gentleness, violence, in comprehensive innocence; but which for those who have known civilization teems with dark and bestial horrors. In this half-light Pentheus at last sees Dionysus 'manifested', his head horned like a bull's. Then the hunter becomes the hunted: and Pentheus goes to his end.

The Bacchae is above all a play to be acted. Even for an audience which comprehends little of its intellectual meaning, it has tremendous dramatic force. There are pitfalls for a producer. He must beware of too much elaborate choreography. If he employs a composer he must keep him strictly under control and not let him try to turn the play into an opera – the words of the Choral Odes must be heard and understood. The Chorus must at first be almost all gentleness, and only gradually reveal their ferocity. Some ironical fun may be had in the Cadmus-Teiresias scene, but again careful control is necessary. Most important of all, in the final scene the horror of the head and body of Pentheus must be played down as far as possible, so that effect is gained by suggestion rather than by sight. Greeks could take far more gruesomeness than should be offered to a modern audience of Greek plays; and if a producer or an audience wants butchery on the stage there are plenty of contemporary playwrights to provide it. The golden rule in any production of Greek drama is, to play it straight and simple, and as far as possible to find the answer to every problem in the text itself.

A word should be said about the style and aims of these particular translations. There is no such thing as a definitive translation of a poetic drama; it is often not possible to say that one version is better or worse than another; a translator's perception is his own perception, and his expression of it in English will be individual in direct proportion to his ability. *Hippolytus* was one of my earliest translations; *The Bacchae* came about two years later, and *Medea* some ten years after that. At first I did not think it possible to render iambic verse into any sort of English blank verse while doing justice to the original clarity and force; I therefore in some degree ignored the formal and poetic elements in Euripides' dialogue, and used prose. Later (after translating Aeschylus, who forced me to practise blank verse) I decided that to abandon metre was to omit unnecessarily an important element in the original work; and found that, for me at any rate, the discipline of verse could enhance, rather than inhibit, both clarity and force. The verse must be of a kind that really involves discipline. Even blank verse, I believe, should on the whole find its justification in a line which makes itself felt as a unit, so that its beginning and its ending mean something. Still more should this be so in lyric verse; here my principle is to make each line (or, shall we say, nine lines out of ten) in itself a unit both of rhythm and of sense. Only if this is done will the member of the audience, listening conscientiously to an unfamiliar *genre*, find that the verse, instead of hindering, actually helps him to absorb at once both meaning and atmosphere.

PHILIP VELLACOTT

MEDEA

CHARACTERS

NURSE
TUTOR *to Medea's sons*
MEDEA
CHORUS *of Corinthian women*
CREON *king of Corinth*
JASON
AEGEUS *king of Athens*
MESSENGER
MEDEA'S TWO CHILDREN

◻

MEDEA

Scene: Before Jason's house in Corinth

NURSE

If only they had never gone! If the Argo's hull
Never had winged out through the grey-blue jaws of rock
And on towards Colchis! If that pine on Pelion's slopes
Had never felt the axe, and fallen, to put oars
Into those heroes' hands, who went at Pelias' bidding
To fetch the golden fleece! Then neither would Medea,
My mistress, ever have set sail for the walled town
Of Iolcus, mad with love for Jason; nor would she,
When Pelias' daughters, at her instance, killed their father,
Have come with Jason and her children to live here
In Corinth; where, coming as an exile, she has earned
The citizens' welcome; while to Jason she is all
Obedience – and in marriage that's the saving thing,
When a wife obediently accepts her husband's will.

But now her world has turned to enmity, and wounds her
Where her affection's deepest. Jason has betrayed
His own sons, and my mistress, for a royal bed,
For alliance with the king of Corinth. He has married
Glauce, Creon's daughter. Poor Medea! Scorned and shamed,
She raves, invoking every vow and solemn pledge
That Jason made her, and calls the gods as witnesses
What thanks she has received for her fidelity.
She will not eat; she lies collapsed in agony,
Dissolving the long hours in tears. Since first she heard

3

Of Jason's wickedness, she has not raised her eyes,
Or moved her cheek from the hard ground; and when her friends
Reason with her, she might be a rock or wave of the sea,
For all she hears – unless, maybe, she turns away
Her lovely head, speaks to herself alone, and wails
Aloud for her dear father, her own land and home,
Which she betrayed and left, to come here with this man
Who now spurns and insults her. Poor Medea! Now
She learns through pain what blessings they enjoy who are not
Uprooted from their native land. She hates her sons:
To see them is no pleasure to her. I am afraid
Some dreadful purpose is forming in her mind. She is
A frightening woman; no one who makes an enemy
Of her will carry off an easy victory.

Here come the boys, back from their running. They've no thought
Of this cruel blow that's fallen on their mother. Well,
They're young; young heads and painful thoughts don't go
together.

Enter the TUTOR *with* MEDEA'S TWO SONS

TUTOR
Old nurse and servant of my mistress's house, tell me,
What are you doing, standing out here by the door,
All alone, talking to yourself, harping on trouble?
Eh? What does Medea say to being left alone?

NURSE
Old friend, tutor of Jason's sons, an honest slave
Suffers in her own heart the blow that strikes her mistress.
It was too much, I couldn't bear it; I had to come
Out here and tell my mistress's wrongs to earth and heaven.

TUTOR
Poor woman! Has she not stopped crying yet?

NURSE   Stopped crying?
I envy you. Her grief's just born – not yet half-grown.

TUTOR
Poor fool – though she's my mistress and I shouldn't say it –
She had better save her tears. She has not heard the worst.

NURSE
The worst? What now? Don't keep it from me. What has
happened?

TUTOR
Why, nothing's happened. I'm sorry I said anything.

NURSE
Look – we're both slaves together: don't keep me in the dark.
Is it so great a secret? I can hold my tongue.

TUTOR
I'd gone along to the benches where the old men play
At dice, next to the holy fountain of Peirene;
They thought I was not listening; and I heard one say
That Creon king of Corinth means to send these boys
Away from here – to banish them, and their mother too.
Whether the story's true I don't know. I hope not.

NURSE
But surely Jason won't stand by and see his sons
Banished, even if he has a quarrel with their mother?

TUTOR
Old love is ousted by new love. Jason's no friend
To this house.

NURSE   Then we're lost, if we must add new trouble
To old, before we're rid of what we had already.

TUTOR

But listen: it's no time to tell Medea this.
Keep quiet, say nothing about it.

NURSE   Children, do you hear
What sort of father Jason is to you? My curse
On – No! No curse; he is my master. All the same,
He is guilty: he has betrayed those near and dear to him.

TUTOR

What man's not guilty? It's taken you a long time to learn
That everybody loves himself more than his neighbour.
These boys are nothing to their father: he's in love.

NURSE

Run into the house, boys. Everything will be all right.
[*The* CHILDREN *move away a little*]
You do your best to keep them by themselves, as long
As she's in this dark mood; don't let them go to her.
I've watched her watching them, her eye like a wild bull's.
There's something that she means to do; and I know this:
She'll not relax her rage till it has found its victim.
God grant she strike her enemies and not her friends!

MEDEA'S *voice is heard from inside the house*

MEDEA

Oh, oh! What misery, what wretchedness!
What shall I do? If only I were dead!

NURSE

There! You can hear; it is your mother
Racking her heart, racking her anger.
Quick, now, children, hurry indoors;
And don't go within sight of her,

Or anywhere near her; keep a safe distance.
Her mood is cruel, her nature dangerous,
Her will fierce and intractable.
Come on, now, in with you both at once.
[*The* CHILDREN *go in, and the* TUTOR *follows*]
The dark cloud of her lamentations
Is just beginning. Soon, I know,
It will burst aflame as her anger rises.
Deep in passion and unrelenting,
What will she do now, stung with insult?

MEDEA [*indoors*]
Do I not suffer? Am I not wronged? Should I not weep?
Children, your mother is hated, and you are cursed:
Death take you, with your father, and perish his whole house!

NURSE
Oh, the pity of it! Poor Medea!
Your children – why, what have *they* to do
With their father's wickedness? Why hate *them*?
I am sick with fear for you, children, terror
Of what may happen. The mind of a queen
Is a thing to fear. A queen is used
To giving commands, not obeying them;
And her rage once roused is hard to appease.

To have learnt to live on the common level
Is better. No grand life for me,
Just peace and quiet as I grow old.
The middle way, neither great nor mean,
Is best by far, in name and practice.
To be rich and powerful brings no blessing;
Only more utterly
Is the prosperous house destroyed, when the gods are angry.

Enter the CHORUS *of Corinthian women*

CHORUS
> I heard her voice, I heard
> That unhappy woman from Colchis
> Still crying, not calm yet.
> Old nurse, tell us about her.
> As I stood by the door I heard her
> Crying inside the palace.
> And my own heart suffers too
> When Jason's house is suffering;
> For that is where my loyalty lies.

NURSE
Jason's house? It no longer exists; all that is finished.
Jason is a prisoner in a princess's bed;
And Medea is in her room
Melting her life away in tears;
No word from any friend can give her comfort.

MEDEA [*still from indoors*]
> Come, flame of the sky,
> Pierce through my head!
> What do I gain from living any longer?
> Oh, how I hate living! I want
> To end my life, leave it behind, and die.

CHORUS
> O Zeus, and Earth, and Light,
> Do you hear the chanted prayer
> Of a wife in her anguish?
> [*Turning to the door and addressing* MEDEA]
> What madness is this? The bed you long for –
> Is it what others shrink from?
> Is it death you demand?

Do not pray that prayer, Medea!
If your husband is won to a new love –
The thing is common; why let it anger you?
Zeus will plead your cause.
Check this passionate grief over your husband
Which wastes you away.

MEDEA

Mighty Themis! Dread Artemis!
Do you see how I am used –
In spite of those great oaths I bound him with –
By my accursed husband?
Oh, may I see Jason and his bride
Ground to pieces in their shattered palace
For the wrong they have dared to do to me, unprovoked!
O my father, my city, you I deserted;
My brother I shamefully murdered!

NURSE

Do you hear what my mistress is saying,
Clamouring to Themis, hearer of prayer,
And to Zeus, who is named guardian of men's oaths?
It is no trifling matter
That can end a rage like hers.

CHORUS

I wish she would come out here and let us see her
And talk to her; if she would listen
Perhaps she would drop this fierce resentful spirit,
This passionate indignation.
As a friend I am anxious to do whatever I can.
Go, nurse, persuade her to come out to us.
Tell her we are all on her side.
Hurry, before she does harm – to those in there;
This passion of hers is an irresistible flood.

NURSE

I will. I fear I shall not persuade her;
Still, I am glad to do my best.
Yet as soon as any of us servants
Goes near to her, or tries to speak,
She glares at us like a mad bull
Or a lioness guarding her cubs.
[*The* NURSE *goes to the door, where she turns*]
The men of old times had little sense;
If you called them fools you wouldn't be far wrong.
They invented songs, and all the sweetness of music,
To perform at feasts, banquets, and celebrations;
But no one thought of using
Songs and stringed instruments
To banish the bitterness and pain of life.
Sorrow is the real cause
Of deaths and disasters and families destroyed.
If music could cure sorrow it would be precious;
But after a good dinner why sing songs?
When people have fed full they're happy already.

The NURSE *goes in*

CHORUS

    I heard her sobbing and wailing,
    Shouting shrill, pitiful accusations
    Against her husband who has betrayed her.
    She invokes Themis, daughter of Zeus,
    Who witnessed those promises which drew her
    Across from Asia to Hellas, setting sail at night,
    Threading the salt strait,
    Key and barrier to the Pontic Sea.

MEDEA *comes out. She is not shaken with weeping,*
but cool and self-possessed

MEDEA

Women of Corinth, I would not have you censure me,
So I have come. Many, I know, are proud at heart,
Indoors or out; but others are ill spoken of
As supercilious, just because their ways are quiet.
There is no justice in the world's censorious eyes.
They will not wait to learn a man's true character;
Though no wrong has been done them, one look – and they hate.
Of course a stranger must conform; even a Greek
Should not annoy his fellows by crass stubbornness.
I accept my place; but this blow that has fallen on me
Was not to be expected. It has crushed my heart.
Life has no pleasure left, dear friends. I want to die.
Jason was my whole life; he knows that well. Now he
Has proved himself the most contemptible of men.

Surely, of all creatures that have life and will, we women
Are the most wretched. When, for an extravagant sum,
We have bought a husband, we must then accept him as
Possessor of our body. This is to aggravate
Wrong with worse wrong. Then the great question: will the man
We get be bad or good? For women, divorce is not
Respectable; to repel the man, not possible.

Still more, a foreign woman, coming among new laws,
New customs, needs the skill of magic, to find out
What her home could not teach her, how to treat the man
Whose bed she shares. And if in this exacting toil
We are successful, and our husband does not struggle
Under the marriage yoke, our life is enviable.
Otherwise, death is better. If a man grows tired
Of the company at home, he can go out, and find
A cure for tediousness. We wives are forced to look
To one man only. And, they tell us, we at home
Live free from danger, they go out to battle: fools!

I'd rather stand three times in the front line than bear
One child.

            But the same arguments do not apply
To you and me. You have this city, your father's home,
The enjoyment of your life, and your friends' company.
I am alone; I have no city; now my husband
Insults me. I was taken as plunder from a land
At the earth's edge. I have no mother, brother, nor any
Of my own blood to turn to in this extremity.

So, I make one request. If I can find a way
To work revenge on Jason for his wrongs to me,
Say nothing. A woman's weak and timid in most matters;
The noise of war, the look of steel, makes her a coward.
But touch her right in marriage, and there's no bloodier spirit.

CHORUS
I'll do as you ask. To punish Jason will be just.
I do not wonder that you take such wrongs to heart.
[CREON *approaches*]
But look, Medea; I see Creon, King of Corinth;
He must have come to tell you of some new decision.

CREON
You there, Medea, scowling rage against your husband!
I order you out of Corinth; take your sons and go
Into exile. Waste no time; I'm here to see this order
Enforced. And I'm not going back into my palace
Until I've put you safe outside my boundaries.

MEDEA
Oh! this is the cruel end of my accursed life!
My enemies have spread full sail; no welcoming shore
Waits to receive and save me. Ill-treated as I am,
Creon, I ask: for what offence do you banish me?

CREON

I fear you. Why wrap up the truth? I fear that you
May do my daughter some irreparable harm.
A number of things contribute to my anxiety.
You're a clever woman, skilled in many evil arts;
You're barred from Jason's bed, and that enrages you.
I learn too from reports, that you have uttered threats
Of revenge on Jason and his bride and his bride's father.
I'll act first, then, in self-defence. I'd rather make you
My enemy now, than weaken, and later pay with tears.

MEDEA

My reputation, yet again! Many times, Creon,
It has been my curse and ruin. A man of any shrewdness
Should never have his children taught to use their brains
More than their fellows. What do you gain by being clever?
You neglect your own affairs; and all your fellow citizens
Hate you. Those who are fools will call you ignorant
And useless, when you offer them unfamiliar knowledge.
As for those thought intelligent, if people rank
You above *them*, that is a thing they will not stand.
I know this from experience: because I am clever,
They are jealous; while the rest dislike me. After all,
I am not so clever as all that.

So you, Creon,
Are afraid – of what? Some harm that I might do to you?
Don't let *me* alarm you, Creon. I'm in no position –
A woman – to wrong a king. You have done me no wrong.
You've given your daughter to the man you chose. I hate
My husband – true; but you had every right to do
As you have done. So now I bear no grudge against
Your happiness: marry your daughter to him, and good luck
To you both. But let me live in Corinth. I will bear
My wrongs in silence, yielding to superior strength.

CREON

Your words are gentle; but my blood runs cold to think
What plots you may be nursing deep within your heart.
In fact, I trust you so much less now than before.
A woman of hot temper – and a man the same –
Is a less dangerous enemy than one quiet and clever.
So out you go, and quickly; no more arguing.
I've made my mind up; you're my enemy. No craft
Of yours will find a way of staying in my city.

MEDEA

I kneel to you, I beseech you by the young bride, your child.

CREON

You're wasting words; you'll never make me change my mind.

MEDEA

I beg you! Will you cast off pity, and banish me?

CREON

I will: I have more love for my family than for you.

MEDEA

My home, my country! How my thoughts turn to you now!

CREON

I love my country too – next only to my daughter.

MEDEA

Oh, what an evil power love has in people's lives!

CREON

That would depend on circumstances, I imagine.

MEDEA

Great Zeus, remember who caused all this suffering!

CREON

Go, you poor wretch, take all my troubles with you! Go!

MEDEA

I know what trouble is; I have no need of more.

CREON

In a moment you'll be thrown out neck and crop. Here, men!

MEDEA

No, no, not that! But, Creon, I have one thing to ask.

CREON

You seem inclined, Medea, to give me trouble still.

MEDEA

I'll go. [*She still clings to him*] It was not *that* I begged.

CREON   Then why resist?
Why will you not get out?

MEDEA   This one day let me stay,
To settle some plan for my exile, make provision
For my two sons, since their own father is not concerned
To help them. Show some pity: you are a father too,
You should feel kindly towards them. For myself, exile
Is nothing. I weep for them; their fate is very hard.

CREON

I'm no tyrant by nature. My soft heart has often
Betrayed me; and I know it's foolish of me now;
Yet none the less, Medea, you shall have what you ask.
But take this warning: if to-morrow's holy sun
Finds you or them inside my boundaries, you die.
That is my solemn word. Now stay here, if you must,

This one day. You can hardly in one day accomplish
What I am afraid of.

Exit CREON

CHORUS

    Medea, poor Medea!
    Your grief touches our hearts.
    A wanderer, where can you turn?
    To what welcoming house?
    To what protecting land?
    How wild with dread and danger
    Is the sea where the gods have set your course!

MEDEA

A bad predicament all round – yes, true enough;
But don't imagine things will end as they are now.
Trials are yet to come for this new-wedded pair;
Nor shall those nearest to them get off easily.

Do you think I would ever have fawned so on this man,
Except to gain my purpose, carry out my schemes?
Not one touch, not one word: yet he – oh, what a fool!
By banishing me at once he could have thwarted me
Utterly; instead, he allows me to remain one day.
To-day three of my enemies I shall strike dead:
Father and daughter; and *my* husband.

I have in mind so many paths of death for them,
I don't know which to choose. Should I set fire to the house,
And burn the bridal chamber? Or creep up to their bed
And drive a sharp knife through their guts? There is one fear:
If I am caught entering the house, or in the act,
I die, and the last laugh goes to my enemies.
The best is the direct way, which most suits my bent:
To kill by poison.

So – say they are dead: what city will receive me then?
What friend will guarantee my safety, offer land
And home as sanctuary? None. I'll wait a little.
If some strong tower of help appears, I'll carry out
This murder cunningly and quietly. But if Fate
Banishes me without resource, I will myself
Take sword in hand, harden my heart to the uttermost,
And kill them both, even if I am to die for it.

For, by Queen Hecate, whom above all divinities
I venerate, my chosen accomplice, to whose presence
My central hearth is dedicated, no one of them
Shall hurt me and not suffer for it! Let me work:
In bitterness and pain they shall repent this marriage,
Repent their houses joined, repent my banishment.

Come! Lay your plan, Medea; scheme with all your skill.
On to the deadly moment that shall test your nerve!
You see now where you stand. Your father was a king,
His father was the Sun-god: you must not invite
Laughter from Jason and his new allies, the tribe
Of Sisyphus. You know what you must do. Besides –
[*She turns to the Chorus*]
We were born women – useless for honest purposes,
But in all kinds of evil skilled practitioners.

CHORUS
    Streams of the sacred rivers flow uphill;
    Tradition, order, all things are reversed:
        Deceit is *men*'s device now,
        Men's oaths are gods' dishonour.
    Legend will now reverse our reputation;
    A time comes when the female sex is honoured;
        That old discordant slander
        Shall no more hold us subject.

Male poets of past ages, with their ballads
Of faithless women, shall go out of fashion;
   For Phoebus, Prince of Music,
Never bestowed the lyric inspiration
   Through female understanding –
   Or we'd find themes for poems,
We'd counter with our epics against man.
Oh, Time is old; and in his store of tales
   Men figure no less famous
   Or infamous than women.

So you, Medea, wild with love,
Set sail from your father's house,
Threading the Rocky Jaws of the eastern sea;
And here, living in a strange country,
Your marriage lost, your bed solitary,
You are driven beyond the borders,
An exile with no redress.
The grace of sworn oaths is gone;
Honour remains no more
In the wide Greek world, but is flown to the sky.
Where can you turn for shelter?
Your father's door is closed against you;
Another is now mistress of your husband's bed;
A new queen rules in your house.

Enter JASON

JASON
I have often noticed – this is not the first occasion –
What fatal results follow from ungoverned rage.
You could have stayed in Corinth, still lived in this house,
If you had quietly accepted the decisions
Of those in power. Instead, you talked like a fool; and now
You are banished. Well, your angry words don't upset *me*;
Go on as long as you like reciting Jason's crimes.

But after your abuse of the King and the princess
Think yourself lucky to be let off with banishment.
I have tried all the time to calm them down; but you
Would not give up your ridiculous tirades against
The royal family. So, you're banished. However, I
Will not desert a friend. I have carefully considered
Your problem, and come now, in spite of everything,
To see that you and the children are not sent away
With an empty purse, or unprovided. Exile brings
With it a train of difficulties. You no doubt
Hate me: but I could never bear ill-will to you.

MEDEA
You filthy coward! – if I knew any worse name
For such unmanliness I'd use it – so, you've come!
You, my worst enemy, come to me! Oh, it's not courage,
This looking friends in the face after betraying them.
It is not even audacity; it's a disease,
The worst a man can have, pure shamelessness. However,
It is as well you came; to say what I have to say
Will ease my heart; to hear it said will make you wince.

I will begin at the beginning. When you were sent
To master the fire-breathing bulls, yoke them, and sow
The deadly furrow, then I saved your life; and that
Every Greek who sailed with you in the Argo knows.
The serpent that kept watch over the Golden Fleece,
Coiled round it fold on fold, unsleeping – it was I
Who killed it, and so lit the torch of your success.
I willingly deceived my father; left my home;
With you I came to Iolcus by Mount Pelion,
Showing much love and little wisdom. There I put
King Pelias to the most horrible of deaths
By his own daughters' hands, and ruined his whole house.
And in return for this you have the wickedness

To turn me out, to get yourself another wife,
Even after I had borne you sons! If you had still
Been childless I could have pardoned you for hankering
After this new marriage. But respect for oaths has gone
To the wind. Do you, I wonder, think that the old gods
No longer rule? Or that new laws are now in force?
You must know you are guilty of perjury to me.

My poor right hand, which you so often clasped! My knees
Which you then clung to! How we are besmirched and mocked
By this man's broken vows, and all our hopes deceived!

Come, I'll ask your advice as if you were a friend.
Not that I hope for any help from you; but still,
I'll ask you, and expose your infamy. Where now
Can I turn? Back to my country and my father's house,
Which I betrayed to come with you? Or to Iolcus,
To Pelias's wretched daughters? What a welcome they
Would offer me, who killed their father! Thus it stands:
My friends at home now hate me; and in helping you
I have earned the enmity of those I had no right
To hurt. For my reward, you have made me the envy
Of Hellene women everywhere! A marvellous
Husband I have, and faithful too, in the name of pity;
When I'm banished, thrown out of the country without a friend,
Alone with my forlorn waifs. Yes, a shining shame
It will be to you, the new-made bridegroom, that your own sons,
And I who saved your life, are begging beside the road!

O Zeus! Why have you given us clear signs to tell
True gold from counterfeit; but when we need to know
Bad *men* from good, the flesh bears no revealing mark?

CHORUS
The fiercest anger of all, the most incurable,
Is that which rages in the place of dearest love.

JASON

I have to show myself a clever speaker, it seems.
This hurricane of recrimination and abuse
Calls for good seamanship: I'll furl all but an inch
Of sail, and ride it out. To begin with, since you build
To such a height your services to me, I hold
That credit for my successful voyage was solely due
To Aphrodite, no one else divine or human.
I admit, you have intelligence; but, to recount
How helpless passion drove you then to save my life
Would be invidious; and I will not stress the point.
Your services, so far as they went, were well enough;
But in return for saving me you got far more
Than you gave. Allow me, in the first place, to point out
That you left a barbarous land to become a resident
Of Hellas; here you have known justice; you have lived
In a society where force yields place to law.
Moreover, here your gifts are widely recognized,
You are famous; if you still lived at the ends of the earth
Your name would never be spoken. Personally, unless
Life brings me fame, I long neither for hoards of gold,
Nor for a voice sweeter than Orpheus! – Well, *you* began
The argument about my voyage; and that's my answer.

As for your scurrilous taunts against my marriage with
The royal family, I shall show you that my action
Was wise, not swayed by passion, and directed towards
Your interests and my children's. – No, keep quiet! When I
Came here from Iolcus as a stateless exile, dogged
And thwarted by misfortunes – why, what luckier chance
Could I have met, than marriage with the King's daughter?
It was not, as you resentfully assume, that I
Found your attractions wearisome, and was smitten with
Desire for a new wife; nor did I specially want
To raise a numerous family – the sons we have

Are enough, I'm satisfied; but I wanted to ensure
First – and the most important – that we should live well
And not be poor; I know how a poor man is shunned
By all his friends. Next, that I could bring up my sons
In a manner worthy of my descent; have other sons,
Perhaps, as brothers to your children; give them all
An equal place, and so build up a closely-knit
And prosperous family. *You* need no more children, do you?
While *I* thought it worth while to ensure advantages
For those I have, by means of those I hope to have.

Was such a plan, then, wicked? Even you would approve
If you could govern your sex-jealousy. But you women
Have reached a state where, if all's well with your sex-life,
You've everything you wish for; but when *that* goes wrong,
At once all that is best and noblest turns to gall.
If only children could be got some other way,
Without the female sex! If women didn't exist,
Human life would be rid of all its miseries.

CHORUS
Jason, you have set your case forth very plausibly.
But to my mind – though you may be surprised at this –
You are acting wrongly in thus abandoning your wife.

MEDEA
No doubt I differ from many people in many ways.
To me, a wicked man who is also eloquent
Seems the most guilty of them all. He'll cut your throat
As bold as brass, because he knows he can dress up murder
In handsome words. He's not so clever after all.
You dare outface me now with glib high-mindedness!
One word will throw you: if you were honest, you ought first
To have won me over, not got married behind my back.

JASON

No doubt, if I had mentioned it, you would have proved
Most helpful. Why, even now you will not bring yourself
To calm this raging temper.

MEDEA   That was not the point;
But you're an ageing man, and an Asiatic wife
Was no longer respectable.

JASON   Understand this:
It's not for the sake of any woman that I have made
This royal marriage, but, as I've already said,
To ensure your future, and to give my children brothers
Of royal blood, and build security for us all.

MEDEA

I loathe your prosperous future; I'll have none of it,
Nor none of your security – it galls my heart.

JASON

You know – you'll change your mind and be more sensible.
You'll soon stop thinking good is bad, and striking these
Pathetic poses when in fact you're fortunate.

MEDEA

Go on, insult me: you have a roof over your head.
I am alone, an exile.

JASON   It was your own choice.
Blame no one but yourself.

MEDEA   *My* choice? What did I do?
Did I make you my wife and then abandon you?

JASON

You called down wicked curses on the King and his house.

MEDEA

I did. On your house too Fate sends me as a curse.

JASON

I'll not pursue this further. If there's anything else
I can provide to meet the children's needs or yours,
Tell me; I'll gladly give whatever you want, or send
Letters of introduction, if you like, to friends
Who will help you. – Listen: to refuse such help is mad.
You've everything to gain if you give up this rage.

MEDEA

Nothing would induce me to have dealings with your friends,
Nor to take any gifts of yours; so offer none.
A lying traitor's gifts carry no luck.

JASON   Very well.
I call the gods to witness that I have done my best
To help you and the children. You make no response
To kindness; friendly overtures you obstinately
Reject. So much the worse for you.

MEDEA   Go! You have spent
Too long out here. You are consumed with craving for
Your newly-won bride. Go, enjoy her!   [*Exit* JASON]
                                    It may be –
And God uphold my words – that this your marriage-day
Will end with marriage lost, loathing and horror left.

CHORUS

    Visitations of love that come
    Raging and violent on a man

Bring him neither good repute nor goodness.
But if Aphrodite descends in gentleness
No other goddess brings such delight.
Never, Queen Aphrodite,
Loose against me from your golden bow,
Dipped in sweetness of desire,
Your inescapable arrow!

Let Innocence, the gods' loveliest gift,
Choose me for her own;
Never may the dread Cyprian
Craze my heart to leave old love for new,
Sending to assault me
Angry disputes and feuds unending;
But let her judge shrewdly the loves of women
And respect the bed where no war rages.

O my country, my home!
May the gods save me from becoming
A stateless refugee
Dragging out an intolerable life
In desperate helplessness!
That is the most pitiful of all griefs;
Death is better. Should such a day come to me
I pray for death first.
Of all pains and hardships none is worse
Than to be deprived of your native land.

This is no mere reflection derived from hearsay;
It is something we have seen.
You, Medea, have suffered the most shattering of blows;
Yet neither the city of Corinth
Nor any friend has taken pity on you.
May dishonour and ruin fall on the man
Who, having unlocked the secrets

Of a friend's frank heart, can then disown him!
He shall be no friend of mine.

Enter AEGEUS

AEGEUS
All happiness to you, Medea! Between old friends
There is no better greeting.

MEDEA   All happiness to you,
Aegeus, son of Pandion the wise! Where have you come from?

AEGEUS
From Delphi, from the ancient oracle of Apollo.

MEDEA
The centre of the earth, the home of prophecy:
Why did you go?

AEGEUS   To ask for children; that my seed
May become fertile.

MEDEA   What! Have you lived so many years
Childless?

AEGEUS Childless I am; so some fate has ordained.

MEDEA
You have a wife, or not?

AEGEUS   I am married.

MEDEA   And what answer
Did Phoebus give you about children?

AEGEUS   His answer was
Too subtle for me or any human interpreter.

MEDEA
Is it lawful for me to hear it?

AEGEUS   Certainly; a brain
Like yours is what is needed.

MEDEA   Tell me, since you may.

AEGEUS
He commanded me 'not to unstop the wineskin's neck' –

MEDEA
Yes – until when?

AEGEUS   Until I came safe home again.

MEDEA
I see. And for what purpose have you sailed to Corinth?

AEGEUS
You know the King of Troezen, Pittheus, son of Pelops?

MEDEA
Yes, a most pious man.

AEGEUS   I want to ask his advice
About this oracle.

MEDEA   He is an expert in such matters.

AEGEUS
Yes, and my closest friend. We went to the wars together.

MEDEA
I hope you will get all you long for, and be happy.

AEGEUS
But you are looking pale and wasted: what is the matter?

MEDEA
Aegeus, my husband's the most evil man alive.

AEGEUS
Why, what's this? Tell me all about your unhappiness.

MEDEA
Jason has betrayed me, though I never did him wrong.

AEGEUS
What has he done? Explain exactly.

MEDEA   He has taken
Another wife, and made her mistress of *my* house.

AEGEUS
But such a thing is shameful! He has never dared –

MEDEA
It is so. Once he loved me; now I am disowned.

AEGEUS
Was he tired of you? Or did he fall in love elsewhere?

MEDEA
Oh, passionately. He's not a man his friends can trust.

AEGEUS
Well, if – as you say – he's a bad lot, let him go.

MEDEA
It's royalty and power he's fallen in love with.

AEGEUS   What?
Go on. Who's the girl's father?

MEDEA   Creon, King of Corinth.

AEGEUS
I see. Then you have every reason to be upset.

MEDEA
It is the end of everything! What's more, I'm banished.

AEGEUS
Worse still – extraordinary! Why, who has banished you?

MEDEA
Creon has banished me from Corinth.

AEGEUS   And does Jason
Accept this? How disgraceful!

MEDEA   Oh, no! He protests.
But he's resolved to bear it bravely. – Aegeus, see,
I touch your beard as a suppliant, embrace your knees,
Imploring you to have pity on my wretchedness.
Have pity! I am an exile; let me not be friendless.
Receive me in Athens; give me a welcome in your house.
So may the gods grant you fertility, and bring
Your life to a happy close. You have not realized
What good luck chance has brought you. I know certain drugs
Whose power will put an end to your sterility.
I promise you shall beget children.

AEGEUS   I am anxious,
For many reasons, to help you in this way, Medea;
First, for the gods' sake, then this hope you've given me
Of children – for I've quite despaired of my own powers.
This then is what I'll do: once you can get to Athens
I'll keep my promise and protect you all I can.
But I must make this clear first: I do not intend
To take you with me away from Corinth. If you come
Yourself to Athens, you shall have sanctuary there;
I will not give you up to anyone. But first
Get clear of Corinth without help; the Corinthians too
Are friends of mine, and I don't wish to give offence.

MEDEA
So be it. Now confirm your promise with an oath,
And all is well between us.

AEGEUS   Why? Do you not trust me?
What troubles you?

MEDEA   I trust you; but I have enemies –
Not only Creon, but the house of Pelias.
Once you are bound by oaths you will not give me up
If they should try to take me out of your territory.
But if your promise is verbal, and not sworn to the gods,
Perhaps you will make friends with them, and agree to do
What they demand. I've no power on my side, while they
Have wealth and all the resources of a royal house.

AEGEUS
Your forethought is remarkable; but since you wish it
I've no objection. In fact, the taking of an oath
Safeguards me; since I can confront your enemies
With a clear excuse; while *you* have full security.
So name your gods.

MEDEA   Swear by the Earth under your feet,
By the Sun, my father's father, and the whole race of gods.

AEGEUS
Tell me what I shall swear to do or not to do.

MEDEA
Never yourself to expel me from your territory;
And, if my enemies want to take me away, never
Willingly, while you live, to give me up to them.

AEGEUS
I swear by Earth, and by the burning light of the Sun,
And all the gods, to keep the words you have just spoken.

MEDEA
I am satisfied. And if you break your oath, what then?

AEGEUS
Then may the gods do to me as to all guilty men.

MEDEA
Go now, and joy be with you. Everything is well.
I'll reach your city as quickly as I can, when I
Have carried out my purpose and achieved my wish.

AEGEUS *clasps her hand and hurries off*

CHORUS
May Hermes, protector of travellers, bring you
Safe to your home, Aegeus; may you accomplish
All that you so earnestly desire;
For your noble heart wins our goodwill.

MEDEA
O Zeus! O Justice, daughter of Zeus! O glorious Sun!

Now I am on the road to victory; now there's hope!
I shall see my enemies punished as they deserve.
Just where my plot was weakest, at that very point
Help has appeared in this man Aegeus; he is a haven
Where I shall find safe mooring, once I reach the walls
Of the city of Athens. Now I'll tell you all my plans:
They'll not make pleasant hearing. [*Medea's* NURSE
has entered; she listens in silence] First I'll send a slave
To Jason, asking him to come to me; and then
I'll give him soft talk; tell him he has acted well,
Tell him I think this royal marriage which he has bought
With my betrayal is for the best and wisely planned.
But I shall beg that my children be allowed to stay.
Not that I would think of leaving sons of mine behind
On enemy soil for those who hate me to insult;
But in my plot to kill the princess they must help.
I'll send them to the palace bearing gifts, a dress
Of soft weave and a coronet of beaten gold.
If she takes and puts on this finery, both she
And all who touch her will expire in agony;
With such a deadly poison I'll anoint my gifts.

However, enough of that. What makes me cry with pain
Is the next thing I have to do. I will kill my sons.
No one shall take my children from me. When I have made
Jason's whole house a shambles, I will leave Corinth
A murderess, flying from my darling children's blood.
Yes, I can endure guilt, however horrible;
The laughter of my enemies I will not endure.

Now let things take their course. What use is life to me?
I have no land, no home, no refuge from despair.
My folly was committed long ago, when I
Was ready to desert my father's house, won over

By eloquence from a Greek, whom with God's help I now
Will punish. He shall never see alive again
The sons he had from me. From his new bride he never
Shall breed a son; she by my poison, wretched girl,
Must die a hideous death. Let no one think of me
As humble or weak or passive; let them understand
I am of a different kind: dangerous to my enemies,
Loyal to my friends. To such a life glory belongs.

CHORUS
Since you have told us everything, and since I want
To be your friend, and also to uphold the laws
Of human life – I tell you, you must not do this!

MEDEA
No other thing is possible. You have excuse
For speaking so: you have not been treated as I have.

CHORUS
But – to kill your own children! Can you steel your heart?

MEDEA
This is the way to deal Jason the deepest wound.

CHORUS
This way will bring you too the deepest misery.

MEDEA
Let be. Until it is done words are unnecessary.
Nurse! You are the one I use for messages of trust.
Go and bring Jason here. As you're a loyal servant,
And a woman, breathe no word about my purposes.

Exit NURSE

CHORUS

The people of Athens, sons of Erechtheus, have enjoyed their
prosperity
Since ancient times. Children of blessed gods,
They grew from holy soil unscorched by invasion.
Among the glories of knowledge their souls are pastured;
They walk always with grace under the sparkling sky.
There long ago, they say, was born golden-haired Harmony,
Created by the nine virgin Muses of Pieria.

They say that Aphrodite dips her cup
In the clear stream of the lovely Cephisus;
It is she who breathes over the land the breath
Of gentle honey-laden winds; her flowing locks
She crowns with a diadem of sweet-scented roses,
And sends the Loves to be enthroned beside Knowledge,
And with her to create excellence in every art.

Then how will such a city,
Watered by sacred rivers,
A country giving protection to its friends –
How will Athens welcome
You, the child-killer
Whose presence is pollution?
Contemplate the blow struck at a child,
Weigh the blood you take upon you.
Medea, by your knees,
By every pledge or appeal we beseech you,
Do not slaughter your children!

Where will you find hardness of purpose?
How will you build resolution in hand or heart
To face horror without flinching?
When the moment comes, and you look at them –
The moment for you to assume the role of murderess –

How will you do it?
When your sons kneel to you for pity,
Will you stain your fingers with their blood?
Your heart will melt; you will know you cannot.

Enter JASON *from the palace*
Two maids come from the house to attend Medea

JASON
You sent for me: I have come. Although you hate me, I
Am ready to listen. You have some new request; what is it?

MEDEA
Jason, I ask you to forgive the things I said.
You must bear with my violent temper; you and I
Share many memories of love. I have been taking
Myself to task. 'You are a fool,' I've told myself,
'You're mad, when people try to plan things for the best,
To be resentful, and pick quarrels with the King
And with your husband; what he's doing will help us all.
His wife is royal; her sons will be my sons' brothers.
Why not throw off your anger? What is the matter, since
The gods are making kind provision? After all
I have two children still to care for; and I know
We came as exiles, and our friends are few enough.'
When I considered this, I saw my foolishness;
I saw how useless anger was. So now I welcome
What you have done; I think you are wise to gain for us
This new alliance, and the folly was all mine.
I should have helped you in your plans, made it my pleasure
To get ready your marriage-bed, attend your bride.
But we women – I won't say we are bad by nature,
But we are what we are. You, Jason, should not copy
Our bad example, or match yourself with us, showing
Folly for folly. I give in; I was wrong just now,

I admit. But I have thought more wisely of it since.
Children, children! Are you indoors? Come out here.
[*The* CHILDREN *come out – their* TUTOR *follows*] Children,
Greet your father, as I do, and put your arms round him.
Forget our quarrel, and love him as your mother does.
We have made friends; we are not angry any more.
There, children; take his hand. [*She turns away
in a sudden flood of weeping*] Forgive me; I recalled
What pain the future hides from us. [*After embracing Jason
the* CHILDREN *go back to Medea*] Oh children! Will you
All your lives long, stretch out your hands to me like this?
Oh, my tormented heart is full of tears and terrors.
After so long, I have ended my quarrel with your father;
And now, see! I have drenched this young face with my tears.

CHORUS
I too feel fresh tears fill my eyes. May the course of evil
Be checked now, go no further!

JASON   I am pleased, Medea,
That you have changed your mind; though indeed I do not blame
Your first resentment. Only naturally a woman
Is angry when her husband marries a second wife.
You have had wiser thoughts; and though it has taken time,
You have recognized the right decision. This is the act
Of a sensible woman. As for you, my boys, your father
Has taken careful thought, and, with the help of the gods,
Ensured a good life for you. Why, in time, I'm sure,
You with your brothers will be leading men in Corinth.
Only grow big and strong. Your father, and those gods
Who are his friends, have all the rest under control.
I want to see you, when you're strong, full-grown young men,
Tread down my enemies. [*Again* MEDEA
breaks down and weeps] What's this? Why these floods of tears?

Why are you pale? Did you not like what I was saying?
Why do you turn away?

MEDEA   It is nothing. I was thinking
About these children.

JASON   I'll provide for them. Cheer up.

MEDEA
I will. It is not that I mean to doubt your word.
But women – are women; tears come naturally to us.

JASON
Why do you grieve so over the children?

MEDEA   I'm their mother.
When you just now prayed for them to live long, I wondered
Whether it would be so; and grief came over me.
But I've said only part of what I had to say;
Here is the other thing. Since Creon has resolved
To send me out of Corinth, I fully recognize
That for me too this course is best. If I lived here
I should become a trouble both to you and him.
People believe I bear a grudge against you all.
So I must go. But the boys – I would like *them* to be
Brought up in your care. Beg Creon to let them stay.

JASON
I don't know if I can persuade him; but I'll try.

MEDEA
Then – get your wife to ask her father to let them stay.

JASON
Why, certainly; I'm pretty sure she'll win him over.

MEDEA

She will, if she's like other women. But I too
Can help in this. I'll send a present to your wife –
The loveliest things to be found anywhere on earth.
The boys shall take them. – One of you maids, go quickly, bring
The dress and golden coronet. – They will multiply
Her happiness many times, when she can call her own
A royal, noble husband, and these treasures, which
My father's father the Sun bequeathed to his descendants.
[*A slave has brought a casket, which* MEDEA
now hands to her sons]
Boys, hold these gifts. Now carry them to the happy bride,
The princess royal; give them into her own hands.
Go! She will find them all that such a gift should be.

JASON

But why deprive yourself of such things, foolish woman?
Do you think a royal palace is in want of dresses?
Or gold, do you suppose? Keep them, don't give them away.
If my wife values me at all she will yield to *me*
More than to costly presents, I am sure of that.

MEDEA

Don't stop me. Gifts, they say, persuade even the gods;
With mortals, gold outweighs a thousand arguments.
The day is hers; from now on *her* prosperity
Will rise to new heights. She is royal and young. To buy
My sons from exile I would give life, not just gold.
Come, children, go both of you into this rich palace;
Kneel down and beg your father's new wife, and my mistress,
That you may not be banished. And above all, see
That she receives my present into her own hands.
Go quickly; be successful, and bring good news back,
That what your mother longs for has been granted you.

Exit JASON *followed by the* CHILDREN *and the* TUTOR

CHORUS
    Now I have no more hope,
    No more hope that the children can live;
    They are walking to murder at this moment.
    The bride will receive the golden coronet,
    Receive her merciless destroyer;
    With her own hands she will carefully fit
    The adornment of death round her golden hair.

    She cannot resist such loveliness, such heavenly gleaming;
    She will enfold herself
    In the dress and the wreath of wrought gold,
    Preparing her bridal beauty
    To enter a new home – among the dead.
    So fatal is the snare she will fall into,
    So inevitable the death that awaits her;
    From its cruelty there is no escape.

    And you, unhappy Jason, ill-starred in marriage,
    You, son-in-law of kings:
    Little you know that the favour you ask
    Will seal your sons' destruction
    And fasten on your wife a hideous fate.
    O wretched Jason!
    So sure of destiny, and so ignorant!

    Your sorrow next I weep for, pitiable mother;
    You, for jealousy of your marriage-bed,
    Will slaughter your children;
    Since, disregarding right and loyalty,
    Your husband has abandoned you
    And lives with another wife.

The TUTOR *returns from the palace with the two* CHILDREN

TUTOR
Mistress! These two boys are reprieved from banishment.
The princess took your gifts from them with her own hand,
And was delighted. They have no enemies in the palace.
[MEDEA *is silent*]
Well, bless my soul!
Isn't that good news? Why do you stand there thunderstruck?

MEDEA [*to herself*]
How cruel, how cruel!

TUTOR   That's out of tune with the news I brought.

MEDEA
How cruel life is!

TUTOR   Have I, without knowing it,
Told something dreadful, then? I thought my news was good.

MEDEA
Your news is what it is. I am not blaming you.

TUTOR
Then why stand staring at the ground, with streaming eyes?

MEDEA
Strong reason forces me to weep, old friend. The gods,
And my own evil-hearted plots, have led to this.

TUTOR
Take heart, mistress; in time your sons will bring you home.

MEDEA
Before then, I have others to send home. – Oh, gods! [*She weeps*]

TUTOR
You're not the only mother parted from her sons.
We are all mortal; you must not bear grief so hard.

MEDEA
Yes, friend. I'll follow your advice. Now go indoors
And get things ready for them, as on other days.
[*Exit* TUTOR – *the* CHILDREN *come to Medea*]
O children, children! You have a city, and a home;
And when we have parted, there you both will stay for ever,
You motherless, I miserable. And I must go
To exile in another land, before I have had
My joy of you, before I have seen you growing up,
Becoming prosperous. I shall never see your brides,
Adorn your bridal beds, and hold the torches high.
My misery is my own heart, which will not relent.
All was for nothing, then – these years of rearing you,
My care, my aching weariness, and the wild pains
When you were born. Oh, yes, I once built many hopes
On you; imagined, pitifully, that you would care
For my old age, and would yourselves wrap my dead body
For burial. How people would envy me my sons!
That sweet, sad thought has faded now. Parted from you,
My life will be all pain and anguish. You will not
Look at your mother any more with these dear eyes.
You will have moved into a different sphere of life.

Dear sons, why are you staring at me so? You smile
At me – your last smile: why? [*She weeps –*
the CHILDREN *go from her a little,*
and she turns to the Chorus] Oh, what am I to do?
Women, my courage is all gone. Their young, bright faces –
I can't do it. I'll think no more of it. I'll take them
Away from Corinth. Why should I hurt *them*, to make

Their father suffer, when I shall suffer twice as much
Myself? I won't do it. I won't think of it again.

What is the matter with me? Are my enemies
To laugh at me? Am I to let them off scot free?
I must steel myself to it. What a coward I am,
Even tempting my own resolution with soft talk.
Boys, go indoors. [*The* CHILDREN *go to the door,
but stay there watching her*] If there is any here who finds it
Not lawful to be present at my sacrifice,
Let him see to it. My hand shall not weaken.

Oh, my heart, don't, don't do it! Oh, miserable heart,
Let them be! Spare your children! We'll all live together
Safely in Athens; and they will make you happy. . . . No!
No! No! By all the fiends of hate in hell's depths, no!
I'll not leave sons of mine to be the victims of
My enemies' rage. In any case there is no escape,
The thing's done now. Yes, now – the golden coronet
Is on her head, the royal bride is in her dress,
Dying, I know it. So, since I have a sad road
To travel, and send these boys on a still sadder road,
I'll speak to them. Come, children; give me your hand, dear son:
Yours too. Now we must say good-bye. Oh, darling hand,
And darling mouth; your noble, childlike face and body!
Dear sons, my blessing on you both – but there, not here!
All blessing here your father has destroyed. How sweet
To hold you! And children's skin is soft, and their breath pure.
Go! Go away! I can't look at you any longer;
My pain is more than I can bear.
[*The* CHILDREN *go indoors*] I understand
The horror of what I am going to do; but anger,
The spring of all life's horror, masters my resolve.

MEDEA *goes to stand looking towards the palace*

CHORUS

    I have often engaged in arguments,
    And become more subtle, and perhaps more heated,
    Than is suitable for women;
    Though in fact women too have intelligence,
    Which forms part of our nature and instructs us –
    Not all of us, I admit; but a certain few
    You might perhaps find, in a large number of women –
    A few not incapable of reflection;

    And this is my opinion: those men or women
    Who never had children of their own at all
    Enjoy the advantage in good fortune
    Over those who are parents. Childless people
    Have no means of knowing whether children are
    A blessing or a burden; but being without them
    They live exempt from many troubles.

    While those who have growing up in their homes
    The sweet gift of children I see always
    Burdened and worn with incessant worry,
    First, how to rear them in health and safety,
    And bequeath them, in time, enough to live on;
    And then this further anxiety:
    They can never know whether all their toil
    Is spent for worthy or worthless children.

    And beyond the common ills that attend
    All human life there is one still worse:
    Suppose at last they are pretty well off,
    Their children have grown up, and, what's more,
    Are kind and honest: then what happens?
    A throw of chance – and there goes Death
    Bearing off your child into the unknown.

Then why should mortals thank the gods,
Who add to their load, already grievous,
This one more grief, for their children's sake,
Most grievous of all?

MEDEA
Friends, I have long been waiting for a message from the palace.
What is to happen next? I see a slave of Jason's
Coming, gasping for breath. He must bring fearful news.

Enter a MESSENGER

MESSENGER
Medea! Get away, escape! Oh, what a thing to do!
What an unholy, horrible thing! Take ship, or chariot,
Any means you can, but escape!

MEDEA   Why should I escape?

MESSENGER
She's dead – the princess, and her father Creon too,
They're both dead, by your poisons.

MEDEA   Your news is excellent.
I count you from to-day my friend and benefactor.

MESSENGER
What? Are you sane, or raving mad? When you've committed
This hideous crime against the royal house, you're glad
At hearing of it? Do you not tremble at such things?

MEDEA
I could make suitable reply to that, my friend.
But take your time now; tell me, how did they die? You'll give
Me double pleasure if their death was horrible.

▣▣

MESSENGER

When your two little boys came hand in hand, and entered
The palace with their father, where the wedding was,
We servants were delighted. We had all felt sorry
To hear how you'd been treated; and now the word went round
From one to another, that you and Jason had made it up.
So we were glad to see the boys; one kissed their hand,
Another their fair hair. Myself, I was so pleased,
I followed with them to the princess's room. Our mistress –
The one we now call mistress in your place – before
She saw your pair of boys coming, had eyes only
For Jason; but seeing them she dropped her eyes, and turned
Her lovely cheek away, upset that they should come
Into her room. Your husband then began to soothe
Her sulkiness, her girlish temper. 'You must not,'
He said, 'be unfriendly to our friends. Turn your head round,
And give up feeling angry. Those your husband loves
You must love too. Now take these gifts,' he said, 'and ask
Your father to revoke their exile for my sake.'
So, when she saw those lovely things, she was won over,
And agreed to all that Jason asked. At once, before
He and your sons were well out of the house, she took
The embroidered gown and put it round her. Then she placed
Over her curls the golden coronet, and began
To arrange her hair in a bright mirror, smiling at
Her lifeless form reflected there. Then she stood up,
And to and fro stepped daintily about the room
On white bare feet, and many times she would twist back
To see how the dress fell in clear folds to the heel.

Then suddenly we saw a frightening thing. She changed
Colour; she staggered sideways, shook in every limb.
She was just able to collapse on to a chair,
Or she would have fallen flat. Then one of her attendants,
An old woman, thinking that perhaps the anger of Pan

Or some other god had struck her, chanted the cry of worship.
But then she saw, oozing from the girl's lips, white froth;
The pupils of her eyes were twisted out of sight;
The blood was drained from all her skin. The old woman knew
Her mistake, and changed her chant to a despairing howl.
One maid ran off quickly to fetch the King, another
To look for Jason and tell him what was happening
To his young bride; the whole palace was filled with a clatter
Of people running here and there.
                            All this took place
In a few moments, perhaps while a fast runner might run
A hundred yards; and she lay speechless, with eyes closed.
Then she came to, poor girl, and gave a frightful scream,
As two torments made war on her together: first
The golden coronet round her head discharged a stream
Of unnatural devouring fire: while the fine dress
Your children gave her – poor miserable girl! – the stuff
Was eating her clear flesh. She leapt up from her chair,
On fire, and ran, shaking her head and her long hair
This way and that, trying to shake off the coronet.
The ring of gold was fitted close and would not move;
The more she shook her head the fiercer the flame burned.
At last, exhausted by agony, she fell to the ground;
Save to her father, she was unrecognizable.
Her eyes, her face, were one grotesque disfigurement;
Down from her head dripped blood mingled with flame; her flesh,
Attacked by the invisible fangs of poison, melted
From the bare bone, like gum-drops from a pine-tree's bark –
A ghastly sight. Not one among us dared to touch
Her body. What we'd seen was lesson enough for us.

But suddenly her father came into the room.
He did not understand, poor man, what kind of death
Had struck his child. He threw himself down at her side,
And sobbed aloud, and kissed her, and took her in his arms,

And cried, 'Poor darling child, what god destroyed your life
So cruelly? Who robs me of my only child,
Old as I am, and near my grave? Oh, let me die
With you, my daughter!' Soon he ceased his tears and cries,
And tried to lift his aged body upright; and then,
As ivy sticks to laurel-branches, so he stuck
Fast to the dress. A ghastly wrestling now began;
He struggled to raise up his knee, she tugged him down.
If he used force, he tore the old flesh off his bones.
At length the King gave up his pitiful attempts;
Weakened with pain, he yielded, and gasped out his life.
Now, joined in death, daughter and father – such a sight
As tears were made for – they lie there.

                                        To you, Medea,
I have no more to say. You will yourself know best
How to evade reprisal. As for human life,
It is a shadow, as I have long believed. And this
I say without hesitation: those whom most would call
Intelligent, the propounders of wise theories –
Their folly is of all men's the most culpable.
Happiness is a thing no man possesses. Fortune
May come now to one man, now to another, as
Prosperity increases; happiness never.

Exit MESSENGER

CHORUS
To-day we see the will of Heaven, blow after blow,
Bring down on Jason justice and calamity.

MEDEA
Friends, now my course is clear: as quickly as possible
To kill the children and then fly from Corinth; not
Delay and so consign them to another hand
To murder with a better will. For they must die,
In any case; and since they must, then I who gave

Them birth will kill them. Arm yourself, my heart: the thing
That you must do is fearful, yet inevitable.
Why wait, then? My accursed hand, come, take the sword;
Take it, and forward to your frontier of despair.
No cowardice, no tender memories; forget
That you once loved them, that of your body they were born.
For one short day forget your children; afterwards
Weep: though you kill them, they were your beloved sons.
Life has been cruel to me.

MEDEA *goes into the house*

CHORUS
Earth, awake! Bright arrows of the Sun,
Look! Look down on the accursed woman
Before she lifts up a murderous hand
To pollute it with her children's blood!
For they are of your own golden race;
And for mortals to spill blood that grew
In the veins of gods is a fearful thing.
Heaven-born brightness, hold her, stop her,
Purge the palace of her, this pitiable
Bloody-handed fiend of vengeance!

All your care for them lost! Your love
For the babes you bore, all wasted, wasted!
Why did you come from the blue Symplegades
That hold the gate of the barbarous sea?
Why must this rage devour your heart
To spend itself in slaughter of children?
Where kindred blood pollutes the ground
A curse hangs over human lives;
And murder measures the doom that falls
By Heaven's law on the guilty house.

A child's scream is heard from inside the house

CHORUS
Do you hear? The children are calling for help.
O cursed, miserable woman!

CHILDREN'S VOICES
Help! help! Mother, let me go!
Mother, don't kill us!

CHORUS
Shall we go in?
I am sure we ought to save the children's lives.

CHILDREN'S VOICES
Help, help, for the gods' sake! She is killing us!
We can't escape from her sword!

CHORUS
O miserable mother, to destroy your own increase,
Murder the babes of your body!
Stone and iron you are, as you resolved to be.

There was but one in time past,
One woman that I have heard of,
Raised hand against her own children.
It was Ino, sent out of her mind by a god,
When Hera, the wife of Zeus,
Drove her from her home to wander over the world.
In her misery she plunged into the sea
Being defiled by the murder of her children;
From the steep cliff's edge she stretched out her foot,
And so ended,
Joined in death with her two sons.

What can be strange or terrible after this?
O bed of women, full of passion and pain,
What wickedness, what sorrow you have caused on the earth!

Enter JASON, *running and breathless*

JASON
You women standing round the door there! Is Medea
Still in the house? – vile murderess! – or has she gone
And escaped? I swear she must either hide in the deep earth
Or soar on wings into the sky's abyss, to escape
My vengeance for the royal house. – She has killed the King
And the princess! Does she expect to go unpunished?

Well, I am less concerned with her than with the children.
Those who have suffered at her hands will make her suffer;
I've come to save my sons, before Creon's family
Murder them in revenge for this unspeakable
Crime of their mother's.

CHORUS   Jason, you have yet to learn
How great your trouble is; or you would not have spoken so.

JASON
What trouble? Is Medea trying to kill me too?

CHORUS
Your sons are dead. Their mother has killed both your sons.

JASON
What? Killed my sons? That word kills me.

CHORUS   They are both dead.

JASON
Where are they? Did she kill them out here, or indoors?

CHORUS
Open that door, and see them lying in their blood.

JASON

Slaves, there! Unbar the doors! Open, and let me see
Two horrors: my dead sons, and the woman I will kill.

JASON *batters at the doors.* MEDEA *appears above the roof,*
sitting in a chariot drawn by dragons, with the bodies of the two
children beside her.

MEDEA

Jason! Why are you battering at these doors, seeking
The dead children and me who killed them? Stop! Be quiet.
If you have any business with me, say what you wish.
Touch us you cannot, in this chariot which the Sun
Has sent to save us from the hands of enemies.

JASON

You abomination! Of all women most detested
By every god, by me, by the whole human race!
You could endure – a mother! – to lift sword against
Your own little ones; to leave me childless, my life wrecked.
After such murder do you outface both Sun and Earth –
Guilty of gross pollution? May the gods blast your life!
I am sane now; but I was mad before, when I
Brought you from your palace in a of land savages
Into a Greek home – you, a living curse, already
A traitor both to your father and your native land.
The vengeance due for your sins the gods have cast on me.
You had already murdered your brother at his own hearth
When first you stepped on board my lovely Argo's hull.
That was your beginning. Then you became my wife, and bore
My children; now, out of mere sexual jealousy,
You murder them! In all Hellas there is not one woman
Who could have done it; yet in preference to them
I married you, chose hatred and murder for my wife –
No woman, but a tiger; a Tuscan Scylla – but more savage.

Ah, what's the use? If I cursed you all day, no remorse
Would touch you, for your heart's proof against feeling. Go!
Out of my sight, polluted fiend, child-murderer!
Leave me to mourn over my destiny: I have lost
My young bride; I have lost the two sons I begot
And brought up; I shall never see them alive again.

MEDEA
I would if necessary have answered at full length
Everything you have said; but Zeus the father of all
Knows well what service I once rendered you, and how
You have repaid me. You were mistaken if you thought
You could dishonour my bed and live a pleasant life
And laugh at me. The princess was wrong too, and so
Was Creon, when he took you for his son-in-law
And thought he could exile me with impunity.
So now, am I a tiger, Scylla? – Hurl at me
What names you please! I've reached your heart; and that is right.

JASON
You suffer too; my loss is yours no less.

MEDEA   It is true;
But my pain's a fair price, to take away your smile.

JASON
O children, what a wicked mother Fate gave you!

MEDEA
O sons, your father's treachery cost you your lives.

JASON
It was not my hand that killed my sons.

MEDEA   No, not your hand;
But your insult to me, and your new-wedded wife.

JASON
You thought *that* reason enough to murder them, that I
No longer slept with you?

MEDEA   And is that injury
A slight one, do you imagine, to a woman?

JASON   Yes,
To a modest woman; but to you – the whole world lost.

MEDEA
I can stab too: your sons are dead!

JASON   Dead? No! They live –
To haunt your life with vengeance.

MEDEA   Who began this feud?
The gods know.

JASON   Yes – they know the vileness of your heart.

MEDEA
Loathe on! Your bitter voice – how I abhor the sound!

JASON
As I loathe yours. Let us make terms and part at once.

MEDEA
Most willingly. What terms? What do you bid me do?

JASON
Give me my sons for burial and mourning rites.

MEDEA
Oh, no! I will myself convey them to the temple

Of Hera Acraea; there in the holy precinct I
Will bury them with my own hand, to ensure that none
Of my enemies shall violate or insult their graves.
And I will ordain an annual feast and sacrifice
To be solemnized for ever by the people of Corinth,
To expiate this impious murder. I myself
Will go to Athens, city of Erechtheus, to make my home
With Aegeus son of Pandion. You, as you deserve,
Shall die an unheroic death, your head shattered
By a timber from the Argo's hull. Thus wretchedly
Your fate shall end the story of your love for me.

JASON
The curse of children's blood be on you!
Avenging Justice blast your being!

MEDEA
What god will hear your imprecation,
Oath-breaker, guest-deceiver, liar?

JASON
Unclean, abhorrent child-destroyer!

MEDEA
Go home: your wife waits to be buried.

JASON
I go – a father once; now childless.

MEDEA
You grieve too soon. Old age is coming.

JASON
Children, how dear you were!

MEDEA
To their mother; not to you.

JASON
Dear – and you murdered them?

MEDEA
Yes, Jason, to break your heart.

JASON
I long to fold them in my arms;
To kiss their lips would comfort me.

MEDEA
Now you have loving words, now kisses for them:
Then you disowned them, sent them into exile.

JASON
For God's sake, let me touch their gentle flesh.

MEDEA
You shall not. It is waste of breath to ask.

JASON
    Zeus, do you hear how I am mocked,
    Rejected, by this savage beast
    Polluted with her children's blood?

    But now, as time and strength permit,
    I will lament this grievous day,
    And call the gods to witness, how
    You killed my sons, and now refuse
    To let me touch or bury them.
    Would God I had not bred them,

Or ever lived to see
Them dead, you their destroyer!

During this speech the chariot has moved out of sight

CHORUS
Many are the Fates which Zeus in Olympus dispenses;
Many matters the gods bring to surprising ends.
The things we thought would happen do not happen;
The unexpected God makes possible;
And such is the conclusion of this story.

HIPPOLYTUS

CHARACTERS

APHRODITE *the goddess of sexual love*
HIPPOLYTUS *bastard son of Theseus*
CHORUS *of huntsmen attending Hippolytus*
SERVANT *of Hippolytus*
CHORUS *of women of Troezen*
NURSE *attending Phaedra*
PHAEDRA *wife of Theseus*
THESEUS *king of Athens and Troezen*
MESSENGER
ARTEMIS *the huntress goddess of virginity*

◳

HIPPOLYTUS

The scene is before the royal palace at Troezen, where Theseus is spending a year of voluntary exile to atone for bloodshed. On one side of the stage is a statue of APHRODITE, *on the other a statue of* ARTEMIS. *In the centre is the door of the palace.*

Enter APHRODITE

APHRODITE
Powerful among mortals, glorious among the gods,
I am Aphrodite, named in heaven The Cyprian.
On earth, from the Eastern shore to the outward ocean of the West,
Over all that see the light of the sun my rule extends.
To those who reverence my powers I show favour,
And throw to the earth those I find arrogant and proud.
For gods too have their pride; and it is their nature
To enjoy receiving honour from the mortal race.
And that my words are true I shall show this very day.
Hippolytus, the son whom the Amazon bore to Theseus,
Who was trained from a child by Pittheus the Severe –
Hippolytus, alone among the inhabitants of Troezen,
Calls me the most pernicious of the heavenly powers;
He abhors the bed of love; marriage he renounces;
Honours Apollo's sister, Artemis daughter of Zeus.
All day with her, the virgin, he ranges the green woods,
With his swift hounds emptying the earth of beasts,
Too fond of company too high for mortal men.
I do not envy them their sport – I have little cause;
But Hippolytus has insulted me and shall suffer for it
This very day. My plans, long laid, are well begun,
And little work remains.

59

                        Two years ago Hippolytus
Left Pittheus' house for Athens, the city of Pandion,
To attend the holy Mysteries and complete his initiation;
And there the noble Phaedra saw him, his father's wife;
And a terrible lust, by my contrivance, captured her heart.
The prince came home to Troezen: Phaedra was Queen of Athens.
There on the Acropolis, on the very Rock of Pallas,
She built a temple of Love looking seaward towards Troezen,
Where her heart wandered with her beloved far away;
Still from that time this temple bears Hippolytus' name.
But Theseus, his hands stained with the blood of the Pallantides,
To purge his guilt, consented to live one year in exile,
And sailed with Phaedra his wife from Athens here to Troezen.
She now, poor wretch, groaning and maddened with the stabs of love,
Is dying, and in silence. No one in the palace knows
Her sickness. But not in secret shall her lust's full course be run.
I will reveal the truth to Theseus; all shall be shown.
This youth, who makes war with me, his own father Theseus
Shall kill with curses, by the power Poseidon King of the Sea
Gave him, that three requests of Theseus should not fail.
Phaedra shall save her honour, but must lose her life;
For I will not yield my rights through regard for her misfortunes,
But my enemies shall pay what they owe till I am satisfied.
Now I'll retire. Here comes Hippolytus, son of Theseus,
Home after his exertions in the hunting field, and with him
His whole pack of followers in full cry at his heels,
Singing hymns to Artemis! Little he knows that Death's gates
Are open now, and to-day's light is the last he shall see.

                        Exit

Enter HIPPOLYTUS *with Huntsmen; also an Old Servant*

HIPPOLYTUS

> Follow, and sing!
> Follow the bright Daughter of Heaven!
> Follow our guardian Maid,
>   Artemis!

HUNTSMEN

> Child of Leto and of Zeus,
> Virgin Goddess Artemis,
> Great and holy, hear our song!
>   Greeting, joyful greeting,
>   Loveliest of maidens!
> You who haunt your kingly father's court,
> Tread at ease the broad sky's golden floor,
>   Loveliest of immortal maids,
>   Joyful greeting, Artemis!

HIPPOLYTUS

Goddess, for you I have twined this crown of flowers, gathered
Fresh from a virgin meadow, where no shepherd dares
To graze his flock, nor ever yet scythe swept,
But bees thread the Spring air over the maiden meadow.
There from the running stream Chastity waters the flowers;
And those whose untaught natures Holiness claims entire
May gather garlands there; and the impure may not.
Dear Mistress, take this flowery band for your bright hair,
Offered with reverent heart. I alone among mortals
Enjoy this honour; I am your companion, speak with you,
Hear your voice; only your face I do not see.
And may the end of my life's course be as the beginning!

SERVANT

My lord! – or, Prince! for only gods must be called lord – would
you accept a word of good advice from me?

HIPPOLYTUS
Of course! I should plainly be a fool if I would not.

SERVANT
Then – you know an old law that is laid down for men –

HIPPOLYTUS
No! What do you mean? Why are you asking me this?

SERVANT
The law that says: Abhor pride and all unfriendliness.

HIPPOLYTUS
Yes; a good law: haughtiness is always a hateful thing.

SERVANT
And surely there is a charm in being open and unreserved?

HIPPOLYTUS
Great charm; great profit too, and with little trouble.

SERVANT
Do you not think this is as true for gods as for men?

HIPPOLYTUS
Why, yes; if our mortal ways are like theirs.

SERVANT
Then why have you no prayer for – a great goddess?

HIPPOLYTUS
Be careful! A word may offend. What goddess do you mean?

SERVANT
She stands here at your own door – Aphrodite!

HIPPOLYTUS
I greet her from far off: I am untainted.

SERVANT
Yet she is great; and her power is known and feared.

HIPPOLYTUS
I have no love for gods worshipped by night.

SERVANT
My son, we must not neglect the honour due to gods.

HIPPOLYTUS
Gods may choose whom they will honour: so may mortals.

SERVANT
May the gods grant you wisdom, and good fortune too!

HIPPOLYTUS
Come, men, we'll go in; it is time for food. A loaded table's a
cheerful sight after hunting. Rub down the horses: when I've had
a good meal I'll take them out with the chariot and exercise them
hard. – Your Aphrodite? No! To me she is nothing at all!

Exit HIPPOLYTUS *with Huntsmen*

SERVANT
The ways of young men are not for us to copy. Queen Aphrodite!
with humble hearts, as befits your servants, we worship you. You
must forgive young blood, and the bold spirit that blurts foolish
words against you. Forget that you heard him speak! You are a
god: and the wisdom of gods must be wiser than men.

Exit

◻◻◻

Enter CHORUS *of Troezenian Women*

CHORUS

You have heard of the rocky fountain
Where water gushes streaming from the heart of the earth,
Where they dip pails in the pool:
A friend of mine was there,
Rinsing rich-coloured clothes in the rill-water
And laying them to dry on the sun-baked rock:
She was the first to tell me about the Queen;

How she pines on a sick bed,
Keeps always within doors,
Clouding her golden head in the fine folds of her veil.
This is the third day, they say,
That her lovely lips refuse the gift of the Earth-Mother,
The innocent body of bread.
What storm is wrecking her life she will not tell;
But she longs to moor in the sad harbour of death.

Hers is no wild ecstasy
Sent by Hecate or Pan,
Mountain-frenzy, Corybantic wandering
By Cybele's power possessed.
Has she sinned, neglecting
Immemorial offerings,
Oil and honey for the Huntress Artemis?
Wrath of gods can range and reach
Every shore and island
Through the salt sea's eddies.

Or is Theseus' heart beguiled?
Is your kingly husband false,
Following pleasure in some slave-girl's secret bed?
Has some traveller from Crete

Sailed with news of sorrow
To our friendly harbour?
Are your kindred torn with trouble far away,
That such bitter anguish
Makes your bed your prison?

But women are always weak, and their ways are strange;
Their very being is a blend of terror and helplessness
At the pains and follies their sex inherits.
I have felt this fear thrill through my own womb;
But I cried to the heavenly helper of all women,
Artemis of the arrows;
And always – the gods be praised! – she came to my deep need.

Look! The old Nurse is coming to the door,
Bringing Queen Phaedra into the fresh air.
Her sad face is more clouded than before.
The Queen! How weak she is, how pale!
I long to know what has so wasted her.

Enter, from the palace, PHAEDRA *supported by the* NURSE
Attendants bring a couch for her

NURSE
Oh, the sickness and pain of this cruel world!
What can I do for you? How can I tell?
Here you are, in the light, under the clear sky;
We have brought your bed from the palace.
It was here that you begged and longed to come;
Soon you will change your mind and fret for your room again.
Each minute cheats you, nothing gives you pleasure;
You hate what you have, and crave for what you have not.
Better to be sick, which is a single trouble,
Than wait on the sick, which troubles both heart and hand.
Man's life from birth to death is sorrow and pain,
With never pause or relief;

And when we are dead, is there a happier world?
Knowledge is hidden from us in clouds and darkness.
Since we can know no other kind of life,
Since the world of the dead is a mystery,
It seems we must blindly love, for what it is worth,
Our little gleam of light,
And follow our foolish course content with tales.

PHAEDRA
Support me, my friends, and lift my head;
The strength of my limbs has melted away.
Hold my white hands, my shapely arms!
This braided veil is a weight on my head –
Off with it! Now let my hair fall round my shoulders.

NURSE
Patience, my child! Lie still, you will tire yourself!
If you are quiet and keep a brave heart
Your illness will be easier to bear.
We are mortal, and so must suffer.

PHAEDRA
If I could kneel by a well-side in the fresh dew
And drink a cupful of clear water!
If I could lie under the poplar-trees
And rest deep in the waving grass!

NURSE
Speak low, child! You must not scatter your words
So loud and recklessly! There are people here!
Your speech careers wildly on wheels of madness.

PHAEDRA
Come, take me! I am going
Out to the hills and the woods, the pine-forests

Where hounds pace after blood
And press close on the spotted deer!
O gods! were I there, shouting to the pack,
Lifting the lance to my hair bright in the wind,
Hurling the barbed blade!

NURSE
What is it, child, you are fretting for?
What are hounds and the hunt to you?
Why so in love with water from a spring?
If you are thirsty,
Here by the palace-wall a stream runs down the hill.

PHAEDRA
Lady of the Salt Mere,
Artemis, lover of bold horsemanship!
O for your level rides,
And the tamed strength of a Thessaly horse under my hand!

NURSE
What next will you say? This is madness, child!
You were craving first
To hunt wild beasts in a mountain glade;
Now, for a horse on the dry sandy track.
Here's a task for a prophet indeed, to guess
What god drives you beside yourself
And strikes your senses from you!

PHAEDRA
What have I done? I have been wandering.
My mind went from me – where? where? I was mad,
A god touched me with madness. Oh, my grief!
Dear Nurse, my veil again; I am ashamed
To think what I have said. Cover my face.
My tears fall down, and I am hot with shame.

To come back to a right mind is agony,
And no less agony to remain mad.
It is best, then, to feel nothing, and so die!

NURSE [*veiling her*]
There, child, there! How soon
Shall my face too be veiled with death?
I have lived long, and learnt much.
Since we must die, it would be better,
In making friends, never to go too far,
Or open the depths of our heart to anyone.
The ties of love ought to lie loosely on us,
Easy to break or bind.
For one heart to endure the pain of two,
As I suffer for her, is a cruel burden.
They say that steadfast devotion
Brings with it more trouble than pleasure,
And is an enemy to life and health.
So I think that in this as in other things
It is best not to go too far;
And any wise man will say the same.

CHORUS
Madam, we see the Queen's distress and are sorry for her; but
what her illness is we cannot understand. We would like to ask
you, her old and trusted servant: will you not tell us?

NURSE
I know nothing. I have questioned her, but she will not speak.

CHORUS
Do you not know how, or when, this trouble first began?

NURSE
The answer is still the same: to all such questions she is silent.

CHORUS
How frail and wasted she looks!

NURSE
No wonder: she has eaten nothing for three days.

CHORUS
Is she out of her mind? Or does she mean to die?

NURSE
She means to die. She is starving herself to death.

CHORUS
Strange that her husband should accept it calmly!

NURSE
She hides her illness from him, tells him she is well.

CHORUS
Does he not look at her face and see for himself?

NURSE
Just now it happens he is away from Troezen.

CHORUS
Can you not compel her to speak? Anything, to discover the cause
of this sickness and these delusions!

NURSE
I have tried everything and achieved nothing; but I want to do my
best, and I will not give up even now. And you, friends, are here
to witness that I am one to stand by my lady in time of trouble.
[*She turns to* PHAEDRA]

Dear child, let us both forget the things we said before. Smooth
away this terrible look from your brow: be my dear daughter!

Don't wander any more – I was wrong to follow you, prying into your thoughts; I will be wiser. Is your sickness something you cannot speak of openly? There are women here to help with remedies. But if your trouble can be told to a man, only speak, and we will consult doctors. Well: not a word? My dear, if I have spoken foolishly, correct me; if well, say you agree. Do not sit there dumb! Speak! One word! Look at me! It is no use. [*She weeps*] All our trouble leads to nothing, and we are as far off as ever; she would not soften before, and still refuses. Listen to me, my lady: be if you will more stubborn than the sea; but what of your sons, if you should die? Who will take their part? They will never inherit their father's palace – no, by Hippolyta, Queen of the riding Amazons! She has a son whom your boys will serve as slaves, a bastard nursing the ambition of his royal birth, one you know well: Hippolytus!

PHAEDRA
No! No!

NURSE
Ha! Does that touch you?

PHAEDRA
You kill me! Nurse, by all the gods I implore you never again to speak of him!

NURSE
There! You are not out of your mind, far from it! And yet you still refuse both to save your own life and to help your children.

PHAEDRA
I love my children; but something else is drowning me in despair.

NURSE
My daughter – your hands are free from blood?

PHAEDRA

My hands are pure; but my heart is defiled.

NURSE

Defiled? What? With some wrong done to you by an enemy?

PHAEDRA

No, no enemy! It is no more his will than mine that he should destroy me.

NURSE

Theseus! Has he done you some injury?

PHAEDRA

No! May I prove as guiltless towards him!

NURSE

What then is this terror that is dragging you to your grave?

PHAEDRA

Leave me to my sin. I do not sin against *you*.

NURSE

I will not leave you if I can help it. If I fail it will be your fault.

PHAEDRA

Will you try to force me? Let my hand go!

NURSE

I will not! I will cling to you until you tell me!

PHAEDRA

Poor soul! The truth would be terrible to you too.

NURSE

What could be worse to me than to see you suffer?

PHAEDRA

To tell you would kill you; but what I am doing is for my honour –

NURSE

If so, to speak of it will add to your honour before the world.

PHAEDRA

– I am finding a way to bring honour out of shame.

NURSE

Then I am right in begging you to tell me – how can you hide it?

PHAEDRA

For the gods' sake leave me and let go my hand!

NURSE

Never, while you refuse what you owe to me!

PHAEDRA

It is true! I owe it. I will tell you what you ask.

NURSE

I will be quiet. Now it is for you to speak.

PHAEDRA

O my mother! What dreadful, pitiful lust raged within you!

NURSE

You mean her lust for the bull? Or what do you mean, my child?

PHAEDRA

And you too, O my sister, whom Dionysus desired – how love made you suffer!

NURSE

Why speak of them? Those tales are best forgotten.

PHAEDRA
The curse that destroyed them I now inherit.

NURSE
You frighten me! What are you going to say now?

PHAEDRA
My misery began with them. It is no new thing.

NURSE
You tell me no more of what I long to hear.

PHAEDRA
The words that you want me to say – if only you could speak them
for me!

NURSE
I am no magician to read hidden thoughts.

PHAEDRA
When they say that one is in love, what do they mean by love?

NURSE
Oh, my child! It is the sweetest of all things – yet full of pain.

PHAEDRA
It seems I have found the pain, but no sweetness.

NURSE
What are you saying? You love a man? What man?

PHAEDRA
Why, who should it be? It is he! The Amazon's son!

NURSE
Hippolytus!

PHAEDRA

You spoke his name, not I.

NURSE

Oh, my child! What are you saying? Oh! you have broken my heart! Oh, friends, how can I bear it? How can I go on living? Oh! this hateful life, this accursed day! [*She collapses to the ground, and the* CHORUS *come to help her*] No! Let me fall, leave me alone; I want to die and be at peace! I am dying, my life is over! . . . What does it mean? Here is a pure-hearted woman, with no desire to do wrong, yet lusting after wickedness against her will! [*Defiantly*] Aphrodite is no goddess! No! She has brought this disaster on Phaedra and on me and on the royal house – she is something more than a goddess – something greater!

CHORUS

Did you hear? Oh, did you hear
The Queen's pitiful cry,
Born of a crueller blow
Than human heart can bear?
Beloved Queen, let me die
Before my heart should know
Your heart's despair!
Oh, Phaedra, daughter of sorrow!
Oh, sorrow, nurse of our race!
Deadly calamity, dragged into sudden light!
How can you live to face,
Hour by hour, the horror that hangs its threat
Over your house, unknown as yet?
The Queen of Love sent you a strange star,
Princess of Crete!
We see now where it will sink and set.

PHAEDRA

Women of Troezen, who live here on the outer threshold of
Peloponnese: I have at times lain long awake in the night, thinking
how other lives than mine have been shattered; and I believe that
such misfortune does not arise from inborn folly, since often those
who suffer are wise and good. But this is how we should regard
the matter: we know and see what is right, yet fail to carry it out.
Some fail through sloth, others through valuing some pleasure
more than goodness; and life offers us many pleasures.

Listen: I will tell you the path my thoughts followed. When love
struck me, I searched for the best way to endure the wound. My
first resolve was to let slip no word, to hide what I suffered; for
there is no trusting the tongue, which knows how to instruct others
in wisdom, but by its own folly invites disaster. Next, I prepared
to endure this madness as I ought, by overcoming it with self-
control. Finally, when I still did not succeed in mastering my love,
I determined that the best plan for me, beyond all contradiction,
was to die.

That is the decision I have taken; that is why I did not choose
to thwart my own purpose with any kind of healing drug. If I do
what is right, I would not wish to hide it, any more than to display
my sins before witnesses. I knew that both the thing I craved, and
the craving itself, was a sin. I knew also, too well, that I was a
woman: a mark for the world's contempt. Whatever woman first
was false to her husband with other men, misery and death destroy
her! It was from noble houses that this plague first spread among
women: when the great choose dishonour, the common herd will
do the same. I hate women whose tongues talk of chastity, who in
secret are bold in every sin! Queen Aphrodite, born from the sea's
purity! how can they look into their husbands' eyes, and not
shudder lest sheltering darkness and guilty walls should speak?

Friends, it is for this I am dying, that I may never be found
guilty of disgracing my husband and my children. I want my sons
to go back to the city of cities, to Athens, and hold their heads high
and speak like free men there, and not blush for their mother. To

live burdened with the secret of a parent's sin will enslave the boldest spirit. Only an upright heart and a clear conscience, they say, give a man strength to wrestle with life; while those whose hearts are evil, sooner or later – as a young girl sees the truth in her glass – so they, when Time holds up his mirror, find their own sin revealed. May I never be found among them!

CHORUS
It is true: virtue, wherever it appears, is a beautiful thing; and the fruit of virtue in this life is a good name.

NURSE
My lady, when I heard what had happened to you, at the first shock I was terrified; now I begin to reflect how foolish I was. In human life second thoughts often prove to be wiser. What has happened to you is nothing extraordinary or hard to understand. The fever of Aphrodite has fastened on you: you are in love. What is strange in that? Why, so are countless others! And do you therefore mean to lose your life for love? Then surely there is a hard road ahead for all lovers now and to come, if their duty is to die!

When Love sweeps on in the fulness of her power, there is no resisting. She steals gently on those who yield to her; but those she finds arrogant and haughty she takes and – what do you suppose? – tramples in the dust! Love rides on clouds and strides through the swollen sea. The whole world was born from Love; she sows every seed; every living creature on earth sprang from that sweet desire which is her gift to us. Those who possess pictures drawn in times past, or who spend their days pursuing the arts – they know that Zeus once lusted for Semele, they know that once the lovely goddess of the glowing dawn stole away Cephalus and took him to live among the gods, because she loved him. Yet Cephalus and she live in the sky, and show no haste to quit the company of gods. Events have proved too strong for them; and they, believe me, are content.

And you: do you refuse to submit? Your father, it seems, should have begotten you upon terms, or looked for other gods, if you're resolved to find fault with the laws of Nature. I ask you: how many good and sensible husbands see their wives unfaithful and look the other way? How many fathers help their love-sick sons to get what they want? Why, the true wisdom for mortals is to keep faults well hidden. A builder doesn't plane and polish the rafters in the roof! and it's not for us mortals to struggle after a tiresome perfection. In any case, how do you think you're going to swim clear of this flood of trouble you've met with? You are mortal, child: if the good you find in life outweighs the ill, you will be extremely fortunate.

My dear daughter, soften your stubborn heart; do not blaspheme! What is it but blasphemy, to wish yourself stronger than a god? You are in love: then bear – and dare – what the god has willed. You are stricken: turn the stroke to your own good. Why, there are spells and soothing charms; we'll find a medicine for you. Trouble may wait a long time for men to mend it, if we women take no hand in the matter.

CHORUS
Her advice is more practical, Phaedra, for your present need; yet you, I feel, are right. Though it may be my approval is harder for you to accept, and more painful to hear, than her reproaches.

PHAEDRA
This is what brings ruin on fine cities and ancient houses – fair speech, too fair by far! Instead of saying what you think will please me, show me a way to save my honour.

NURSE
This is mere high-flown talk. Fine sentiments will not help you: you must have your man! He must be told in plain words what has happened, and won over without delay. If this were not a matter of life and death, if you were still a chaste-minded woman,

I would never encourage you so far for your own lust and pleasure; but now we must fight for your life – and there is nothing wrong in this.

PHAEDRA
Nothing wrong! It is horrible! Be silent, never speak such shameful words again!

NURSE
Shameful – maybe; but more use to you than good words. Better do what I say, and live, than die for a vain boast of chastity.

PHAEDRA
No, for the gods' sake! What you say is plausible, but vile. Go no further! I have disciplined my heart to endure this. If you are so eloquent for evil, I shall fall now into the very pit I shrink from.

NURSE
If you feel so, you should not have sinned at heart. Well, you did: now obey me – and be as ungrateful as you like. I have indoors a drug for the soothing of love – I have only now thought of it; it will bring you into no disgrace, no distress of mind, but it will cure you of your passion, if only you are not faint-hearted.

PHAEDRA
This drug – is it an ointment, or a draught?

NURSE
I don't know. Look for help, my girl, not explanations.

PHAEDRA
You may be too clever, and ruin me. I dread it.

NURSE
Then you would dread anything. What is it you are afraid of?

PHAEDRA

Of your saying any word about me to Hippolytus.

NURSE

Leave that to me, child. I know what to do. [*Aside*] Great Queen
Aphrodite, only stand by me now, and help! For what else I have
in mind, a word to our friend in the palace will be enough.

Exit NURSE – PHAEDRA *remains*

CHORUS

    O Love, immortal Power,
Love, dropping desire like dew on yearning eyes,
    Love, whose triumphant arms
Ravish the conquered soul with sweetest ecstasy!
    Come not in cruelty,
Never with ruthless violence invade my life!
    Fiery stroke of star or sun
Is less to fear than Aphrodite's dart
Which flies from the hand of Love, the child of Zeus,
    To madden a mortal heart.

    In vain by Alpheus' banks,
In vain at the Pythian shrine shall sacrifice multiply,
    And the blood of bulls pour forth,
Toll from the pastures of Greece to Apollo and Artemis;
    While Eros, Master of man,
    Who holds Aphrodite's key
    To her chamber of sweet delight,
    Him in our prayers we slight:
Love, whose coming has brought, since the world began,
    Death and calamity!

Iole, Princess of Oechalia,
Was once a free and taintless virgin,

A maiden unmatched with man;
But Aphrodite tore her from her home,
A wild nymph, helpless and frantic;
And there, amidst blood and smoke,
With dying groans for her bridal-hymn,
Gave her to the son of Alcmene
To carry weeping across the sea.

O holy wall of Thebes,
O lips of the Dircean spring,
You with one voice could tell
How terrible is the advent of Aphrodite!
When upon Semele thunder and flame descended,
And her womb gave birth to Bacchus, the child of Zeus,
Aphrodite laid her to sleep,
A bride in the bed of Death.
For the breath of her terror is felt in every land,
And swift as a bee's flight
Is the path of her power.

PHAEDRA
Women, be quiet! . . . Oh, the last blow has fallen!

CHORUS
We will be quiet. But what can this mean?

PHAEDRA
Wait! I want to hear exactly what they are saying.

CHORUS
Something terrible is happening in the palace. Phaedra, what is it?

PHAEDRA
Oh! Why must I suffer so? It is unbearable!

CHORUS
>   What is unbearable?
>   What is this anguished cry?
>   Tell us, what fearful word
>   Fell on your ears like Fate?

PHAEDRA
It is – my death! Come, stand near the door and listen. Do you
hear what an uproar is rising there?

CHORUS
>   You are beside the door:
>   For you the house utters a voice! Tell me, then,
>   What horror you heard,
>   Tell me, what has been done?

PHAEDRA
It is the son of the riding Amazon, Hippolytus, cursing and abus-
ing my old servant.

CHORUS
>   Yes, I can hear the sound,
>   Yet not a word is clear!
>   How can I tell? Oh, it was clear to you,
>   The cry that came from the house!

PHAEDRA
Ah, listen! Yes, too clear! He calls her 'filthy bawd', damns her
for treason to her master's bed!

CHORUS
>   No, no! What shall we do?
>   Lady, you are betrayed!
>   What plan can I offer?
>   Your secret shown to the world,
>   Your life and hope laid in the dust by the hand of a friend!

◨◧

PHAEDRA

She has told him the fatal truth about me. She did it for love, to cure my suffering; but it was wrong!

CHORUS

What now? What way out is there? What will you do?

PHAEDRA

I do not know – only this: that to die at once is the sole escape from this torture.

Enter HIPPOLYTUS, *followed by the* NURSE

HIPPOLYTUS

O Mother Earth! O unfolding radiance of the sun! What things I have heard! What words unspeakable have been spoken!

NURSE

Be quiet, lad, or someone will hear this clamour!

HIPPOLYTUS

How can I be quiet after what I have listened to?

NURSE

I beg you, I kiss your hand – dear boy, be quiet!

HIPPOLYTUS

Keep your hands off my clothes! You shall not touch me.

NURSE

For the gods' sake, have pity! Don't tell what I said to you! It would kill me.

HIPPOLYTUS

Kill you? Your words were harmless, you said!

NURSE
What I said, my son, was not for everyone to hear.

HIPPOLYTUS
Honest words should not be hushed up: let everyone hear!

NURSE
My boy, do not slight the oath you swore me!

HIPPOLYTUS
My tongue swore: the oath does not bind my heart.

NURSE
What will you do, child? Destroy your friend?

HIPPOLYTUS
Friend? God forbid I should have any such friend!

NURSE
Forgive! We are human; we cannot help doing wrong.

HIPPOLYTUS
O Zeus! Why have you plagued this world with so vile and
worthless a thing as woman? If it was your pleasure to plant a
mortal stock, why must women be the renewers of the race?
Better that men should come to your temples and put down a
price, each what he could afford – buy themselves children in
embryo for gold or silver and get their money's worth; then they
could live at home like free men, without women!

Why, for proof that woman is an evil pest – her father, after
begetting and bringing her up, pays out a dowry to find her a
home, and so gets rid of her; while whoever welcomes the viper to
his bosom gleefully decks her out with gauds and gowns like a
sacred statue, heaping beauty upon hatefulness, poor wretch, and
squanders his inheritance. What choice has he? If he marries

noble blood, he beds with his shrew and makes the best of it; or
if he finds a good wife in a worthless family, with that much
comfort he counters his ill-luck. For an easy life, marry a nobody,
and keep her worthless and witless on a pedestal. I hate a woman
who is clever – a woman who thinks more than becomes a woman;
I would not have her in my house! For passion engenders wickedness the more readily in clever women; while the simple are kept
from wantonness by lack of wit.

A wife should have no servant ever come near her, she should
live attended by dumb savage beasts, who could neither understand
her nor speak to her. As it is, unchaste wives sit at home scheming
lechery, while their servants traffic their schemes out to the world –
you for one, coming like a she-devil to invite me to incest with my
father's wife! I'll flush your filthy words from my ears with floods
of water! Do you think I could so sin, when I feel polluted merely
by hearing you?

Listen: I let you trap me into swearing silence. I fear the gods,
and that saves you; otherwise I would at once have told my father
the whole story. Instead, I shall now leave the palace until he
comes back; and I shall say nothing; but I shall come back with
my father, and then I shall observe how you and your mistress
meet his eye. You at least will brazen it out – I know what you're
made of. – Curse the whole race of you! I can never hate you
enough. Ha! They tell me I always say the same thing: well,
women, it seems, always *are* the same thing. So whoever can teach
women to be chaste may forbid me to tread their name in the dust!

Exit

CHORUS
    How cruel a curse it is to be born a woman!
    Who would not pity us?
    What shift, what turn, what plea,
    After the first faltering,
    Can loose us from the clamp of guilt?

PHAEDRA

    I have met what I deserved.
    Earth and sunlight, show me where to fly
    Out of the clutch of Fate!
    Where can I hide my anguish?
    What god or man can give to my guilty soul
    Safety or help or counsel?
    I am caught in toils of torment;
    There is no escape for the living:
    I sink under the scourge of Chance.

CHORUS

Lady, I weep with you. The harm is done; your servant's plans
have failed disastrously.

PHAEDRA [*to* NURSE]

You vile, treacherous murderess, see what you have done to me!
May Zeus who gave me life blast you with fire and grind you to
dust! Did I not try to prevent what you were plotting? Did I not
forbid you to speak a word of what now drags me in the dirt? You
spoke: and your treason robs even my death of honour. Now –
some new plan. Hippolytus, white-hot with rage, will carry your
foul words to his father and denounce me; go complaining to old
Pittheus, fill the whole land with his outrageous tale! Curse you!
Curse all officious fools who thrust their wicked help on their
friends to ruin them!

NURSE

My lady, I have done you wrong; you may well blame me. The
wound pricks, and overcomes your judgment. Yet, if you'll listen
to me, I can speak for myself. I nursed you; I am your friend; I
tried to find a remedy for your trouble; and I was unlucky. With
better luck, I would have been called a wise woman. After all,
wisdom is only happening to guess right.

PHAEDRA

So! This is your just amends to me – to follow up your treachery with argument!

NURSE

We are wasting time in talk. I admit I was unwise; but, my daughter, there's hope, there's life, even now!

PHAEDRA

Stop! Not another word! You gave me advice before, and help too; and both were wicked. Get out of my sight! Scheme for your own affairs, and I will set mine in order!

Exit NURSE

Noblewomen of Troezen, I ask you to do me this favour: bury deep in silence all that you have heard here to-day.

CHORUS

By holy Artemis, daughter of Zeus, I swear to disclose nothing of what has happened to you.

PHAEDRA

That is well. Listen, my friends – I have said this before: I have a remedy for my present plight; one that will ensure an honourable future for my sons, and help me in face of to-day's calamity. The royal house of Crete shall forfeit no reputation through me. After this shame, to face Theseus would be too high a price for one life.

CHORUS

What are you going to do, that is so dreadful and so final?

PHAEDRA

To die. By what means, I will decide for myself.

CHORUS
In God's name, no!

PHAEDRA
You too must school me; I know my part. To-day I'll be rid of life,
and give joy to my immortal murderess. Love is without mercy:
I shall die defeated. Yet my death shall be a curse on another's
life, and teach him not to trample on my agony. He shall have an
equal share in my suffering, and learn to be gentle!

Exit PHAEDRA

CHORUS
    O to escape and hide
High among steep and secret rocks!
    At the touch of a god to change,
    To rise as a bird and ride
On feathered wings among soaring flocks!
    To wander far and free
Where the lost waters of Eridanus flow deep
    Down to an unknown sea;
Where for dead Phaethon the Sun's daughters weep,
      Dropping piteous tears that gleam
      Like amber in the purple stream!

And O for that quiet garden by the Western sea
    Where the daughters of Evening sing
    Under the golden apple-tree;
    Where the bold sailor wandering
    Finds the Ocean-god has barred
His Westward path over the purple waste!
    Where huge Atlas lives to guard
    The solemn frontiers of the sky;
Where in Zeus' palace fountains of ambrosial wine
    Flow by the festal couch divine,

While holy Earth heaps high
Her fruits of rarest taste
To bless the immortal feast with bountiful supply!

White-winged Cretan ship,
That brought my lady Phaedra from her wealthy home
Over the salt swell of the pounding sea –
White sails for the joy of a bride,
To veil the black fate waiting!
Heavy with omen was her course
From Crete to Athens, queen of mainland cities,
When at Peiraeus her seamen leapt ashore
And looped their plaited hawsers on the quay;
Dark again was the hour
When from the rocky harbour of Munychion
The royal progress parted for Troezen.

Thence on Phaedra fell the fatal curse,
When Aphrodite with a cruel unholy lust
Shattered her helpless heart!
Now the storm of her distress
Drives her, a sinking wreck,
Alone to her marriage-chamber.
From the high beam she will tie
Close round her white neck the noose:
This her one choice, to die!
Thus with reverence learnt for her immortal enemy,
And prizing a fair name above her life,
She will win release of heart from her tormenting love.

A voice is heard shouting from the palace

VOICE

Oh, help, help! Anyone who is in the house, come and help! She
is hanging – the Queen, the wife of Theseus!

CHORUS

Oh! She has kept her word! Oh, Phaedra, Phaedra! She is dead, dead! the Queen! Hung high in a strangling rope!

VOICE

Come quickly! Bring a knife, a sword, anything to cut this cord from her neck!

CHORUS

A. Friends, what shall we do? Ought we to go inside and untie the noose and free her?
B. Why, where are the young men who attend her? It is never safe to interfere.

VOICE

Poor lady, she is dead! Lay her limbs out straight. Oh, what a tale to have to tell my master!

CHORUS

Did you hear? Poor Phaedra, she is dead; they are already laying out her body.

Enter THESEUS, *attended by the royal guard. His head is crowned with the garland worn by those who have received a favourable answer from an oracle.*

THESEUS

Tell me, women, what was that outcry in the palace? What I heard was the voices of servants weeping. [*There is silence*] This is strange: I return home from a solemn mission of piety – and my home receives me with shut doors, not a word of welcome or greeting! . . . I hope nothing has happened to Pittheus? He is well advanced in years; yet his departure from this house would be a grief to me.

CHORUS

What has happened, Theseus, has not touched the old. It is the young whose death will break your heart.

THESEUS

What? Is one of my children's lives stolen from me?

CHORUS

No, it is still more terrible: their mother is dead.

THESEUS

What do you say? My wife dead? What happened?

CHORUS

She made a noose with a rope and hanged herself.

THESEUS

But why? Was it some numbing stroke of grief? What could cause so dreadful an act?

CHORUS

That is all I know, Theseus. I have just now come to the palace to mourn for your loss.

THESEUS

Phaedra – dead! . . . Why have I crowned my head with this garland of leaves? *Here* is my answer from the oracle! – Ho, there! Servants! Unbar the doors and open! Open them wide, let me see my dead wife, whose death is death to me!

The doors open, showing PHAEDRA *dead*

CHORUS

Weep for the Queen, tears for her tears!
Phaedra, your agony and your act alike
Must banish peace from this house!

How could you dare a death so hideous, so unholy,
A prey to your own pitiless hand?
Poor soul, what power dims your brightness in death?

THESEUS

O the torture of life! In this city of exile
I have seen surely the utmost of the grief appointed for me!
O Fate, like a cruel heel crushing me and my house,
A nameless foul infection from some pursuing fiend,
Corrupting, annihilating life and the love of life!
I strain despairing eyes over my sea of misery,
And my hope of safety vanishes, for the shore is out of sight
And life is a mounting wave I have not strength to surmount.
    What reason, Phaedra, what malicious chance,
    What fated cruelty can I accuse?
    As a bird from my hand you have vanished,
Swooped swift and daring into the pit of darkness
And left me tears for your death and anguish for your despair!
    Far from here this harvest grew;
    Long ago a sin was sown;
        Fruit the gods have ripened
        For my grief I gather.

CHORUS

King, this sorrow falls not on your soul alone:
    Many share it, weeping
    A dear wife departed.

THESEUS

To go into the dark! Now let me die, and pass
To the world under the earth, into the joyless dark!
Since you, dearer than all, are at my side no longer,
And the death you have dealt is more than the death that has
swallowed you.
Who will tell me the truth? Whence, my wife, could it come –

This chance, whose murderous blow fell on your tortured heart?
What happened? Shall I be told? Or does my palace harbour
A horde of lying lackeys? Phaedra! my heart is broken!
Friends, pity me, who have lived to see such pain
Ravage my home! No words can speak of it,
No human heart bear it. My life is over.

> Now my house is desolate,
> And my children motherless.
> You, the dearest, best, of all
> That the dazzling sun surveys
> Or the star-eyed evening –
> You are gone for ever!

As THESEUS *has been speaking, the* CHORUS *have noticed a letter
tied to* PHAEDRA'S *wrist.*

CHORUS
Theseus, I pity you for the storm that wrecks your home.
Yet, while I have watched your sorrow with tear-filled eyes,
Still I tremble with deeper dread for the terror to come!

THESEUS
Look! Look here! A letter fastened to her dear hand! What does
this mean? Will it tell me something new? Surely, she has written
her dying wishes, begging me to remember our marriage and our
children. Rest easy, Phaedra! My house and bed shall never be
entered by another woman! See, the impression of her golden
signet brings me her greeting from the dead! Now to untwist the
cord from the seal, and see what this letter has to tell me.

CHORUS

> Here is a crueller pain, a deeper horror
> Sent by the gods to crown the rest! If it were I,
> Knowing the truth, how could I bear my life?
> The royal house heaped in ruin, never to rise!
> Gods have pity! Strike not down!

 Hear and help us! . . . In his eyes,
   See, so grimly staring,
   Portents of disaster!

THESEUS

Oh, oh! Horror upon horror, blow upon blow!
Beyond endurance, beyond speech! Oh!

CHORUS

What now? If it is for us to hear, tell us!

THESEUS

The letter! It shrieks, it howls, horrors indelible!
I am crushed; where can I escape? What I have seen has killed me.
A voice from the letter speaks, and tells – what things! what things!

CHORUS

What are you saying, Theseus? Something dreadful must follow.

THESEUS

A thing so dreadful that I scarcely can force my tongue
To utter it. Yet I will speak now. Listen, O city!

   Hippolytus has braved the holy eye of Zeus and violated my
wife's honour!

   Yes, Poseidon my father, you promised me three curses: with
one of them strike down my son! If they were good curses you
gave me, let him not live out this day!

CHORUS

My lord, in heaven's name, take your prayer back! You are
wrong – you will know it later; only trust me!

THESEUS

There is no taking back. I will not only curse but banish him from
the land. If the one fails he shall feel the other. Either Poseidon

⊡⊡

will honour my curse and send his corpse below, or else as a stranger wandering the earth, an outcast from his country, he shall drain his despicable life to the dregs.

CHORUS
Why, look! Here, this very moment, comes your son himself, Hippolytus! King Theseus, calm this dangerous anger, and consider what will be best for yourself and your family.

Enter HIPPOLYTUS, *with Huntsmen*

HIPPOLYTUS
Father, I heard your outcry and came at once. What trouble has caused your distress I do not know; but I wish you would tell me. . . . Oh! What do I see? It is your wife, Father – dead! Dead? How is it possible? I had only just left her; a short time ago she was alive! What has happened to her? How did she die? . . . Father, I am asking you to tell me! Will you not speak? This is no time to be silent! I know that to insist out of season on being told everything is called idle curiosity; but I am a friend – something more than a friend. Surely, Father, you should not hide trouble from me!

THESEUS
Oh, the futile folly of men! Why do they teach arts innumerable, contrive and search out every other thing – when one knowledge they cannot win, one quarry they have not caught: the skill to teach wisdom to the brutish.

HIPPOLYTUS
He would certainly be a clever instructor who could drive sense into a fool. But, Father, this is not the time for philosophical discourse. Sorrow, I fear, is making you talk wildly.

THESEUS

Oh, there should be somewhere a touchstone of human hearts, which men could trust to tell them the truth about their friends, who is loyal and who treacherous! Every man should have two voices, the one truthful, the other – natural; so that his lying voice might be refuted by the true; and we should not be duped.

HIPPOLYTUS

What? Has one of your friends contrived to slander me to you and make you suspect my innocence? I am bewildered, astonished! Your words are crazed, you have taken leave of your wits!

THESEUS

The heart of man! Is there any vileness it will turn from? Will barefaced wickedness ever find its limit? If crime is to bulk bigger with each new generation, new depths of villainy be revealed age after age, the gods will need to create a second earth to house liars and lechers. Look at this man! my own son, who would pollute my marriage-bed – and is proved guilty by the damning witness of her dead hand. Come, show your face – foul as you are, look your father in the eyes! So you – you are the man above men who keeps the company of gods! Yours is the chaste life unsmirched with evil! Who believes your bragging? Who charges gods with such ignorance and folly? Not I! So, now flaunt your purity! Play the quack with your fleshless diets! Take Orpheus for your lord and prophet and wallow in frenzied adoration of his wordy vapourings! Yes, you are exposed! Of such men let the world take warning and beware! They pursue their prey with lofty words and low cunning. – Oh, she is dead: do you think that will save you? No, vile criminal, it is the prime evidence of your guilt. What oaths or arguments could outweigh her witness and acquit you? You will say that she hated you; that there will always be war between the bastard and the true-born. Was she so poor a bargainer with her life, that she would throw away all its sweetness to spite you? Or will you tell me that young men are free from folly, women born to it? Well I know that young men are no steadier than women, when Aphrodite stirs the hot blood in them. Indeed, their sex makes them even more headstrong.

Ah! why should I fight down your defence, when her dead body blazons its evidence to my eyes? Out of this land to exile! Go, I say! Never come near the god-built walls of Athens, cross no frontier that my sword guards! I tell you, if I weaken before this outrage, the Isthmian bandit Sinis shall deny that I killed him, and call me boaster; and the sea-washed rocks where Sciron met his end shall forget the weight of my hand against evildoers!

CHORUS
How can any mortal man be called happy? Until to-day, Hippolytus, you were first in good fortune: now everything is reversed.

HIPPOLYTUS
Father, your passionate anger is terrible; and though what you say at first appears just, you will find it does not bear closer scrutiny. Though I have no skill to address a crowd, among a few equals I can speak with more confidence. And this is natural; just as those who seem fools among wise men can be eloquent before crowds. So, now that my whole life is in danger, I must be bold and speak.

And I will begin with the first charge you levelled at me, which you thought would leave me shattered and speechless. Look at this sky, this earth: in the length and breadth of them there is no man – deny it as you will – more pure in heart than I! I have learnt, first, to reverence the gods; then, to choose friends who keep their hands innocent, whose honour forbids them either to render me or expect from me any discreditable service. I do not mock those I live among, Father; I am the same to my friends absent or present. One act you now think me convicted of is unknown to me: to this day my body is chaste; I have not touched a woman. I know nothing of such matters, more than I have heard men tell, or seen in pictures; which I have little desire to look at, for my mind is virgin. Perhaps you refuse to believe that I am pure: then it is for you to show what temptation was too strong for me. Was your wife more beautiful than all other women? Or did I hope, by winning her love, to become your heir? Any such hope would have been less vain than mad! Did I covet your place as king? For a wise man a throne has no attraction; to find pleasure in power is to be corrupted by it – there are many examples. No; my ambition is a different one: let me be first in the Grecian Games, and in politics take second place, and be happy with honest friends. In this way I am able to live my own life – and to live free from danger, which is a greater blessing than a crown.

That is all I have to say, except one thing: if a witness to my innocence were here to speak, and if Phaedra were alive to listen to my defence, then the event would guide your search for the guilty. As things are, I swear to you by Zeus, Guardian of oaths, and by the Earth, that I never touched your wife, never could have wished even to think of it. I pray that I may die in nameless dishonour, cityless, homeless, exile and vagabond – may neither sea nor land receive my dead flesh, if there is sin in me! Whether it was fear that made Phaedra take her life I do not know; further than this it is impossible for me to speak. She kept her chastity, without possessing the virtue of chastity; I possess it, and have practised it to my own ruin.

CHORUS
Surely what you have said will suffice to clear you! Your solemn oaths to the gods must be believed.

THESEUS
Is he not a spellmonger, a cheat, hoping to master my mind with his smooth temper, after putting his father to open shame?

HIPPOLYTUS
It is *your* smooth temper that I wonder at, Father. If you were my son, and I in your place, I would have killed you, not corrected you with exile, if you had dared to touch my wife.

THESEUS

Indeed! How justly! No, you shall not die like that. Many a criminal would be glad of a quick death. No: since you have passed sentence on yourself, you shall wander an outcast from your country, on alien soil you shall drain the bitter lees of life, and earn a criminal's reward.

HIPPOLYTUS

What? You will do that? You will not wait for the witness of time to condemn me, but drive me out to-day?

THESEUS

Yes! beyond the outer ocean and the ends of the earth, if I had the power, so abominable to me is the sight of you!

HIPPOLYTUS

You spurn my sworn oath, you seek no guidance of priests, but banish me unjudged?

THESEUS

Priests! with their omens from birds that fly about overhead! To me they are nothing at all! This letter here is no soothsayer's riddle, and it proves you guilty.

HIPPOLYTUS

Why do I not unlock my lips? You gods, whom my silence honours, it is you who destroy me! – No: I will not speak. Nothing I might say now could carry weight where it would help me. To tell the truth would be to break my oath and gain nothing.

THESEUS

Still your cursed piety! It chokes me! What are you waiting for? Out of my land, I say!

HIPPOLYTUS

Out of your land? Which way shall I turn? Who of my friends will receive me, exiled on such a charge?

THESEUS

Who? Any that has a warm welcome for the defiler of men's wives, the bosom-friend of all iniquity!

HIPPOLYTUS

Oh, it is time indeed for tears and a broken heart, when my father thinks and truly believes that I am guilty.

THESEUS

The time for you to weep and be wise was the time when you cast off shame to dishonour your father's wife!

HIPPOLYTUS

Oh, if these walls could but cry out and speak for me, and witness whether I am so vile a man!

THESEUS

You are careful to fly for help to dumb witnesses; but the fact needs no tongue to prove you guilty.

HIPPOLYTUS

I wish for very pity that I could stand apart and behold myself, to shed tears for my own suffering!

THESEUS

No doubt! You are far more practised in self-worship than in self-control and honourable conduct to your father.

HIPPOLYTUS

My unhappy mother! I was born in bitterness of sorrow. May no one that I love ever be called bastard!

THESEUS

Guards! take him away! Do you not hear? I have already pronounced him banished.

HIPPOLYTUS

It will be the worse for any of them that touches me. Since you're so minded, thrust me out yourself!

THESEUS

I will do so, unless you obey me. Your exile does not touch my tears.

Exit THESEUS

HIPPOLYTUS

My fate, then, is fixed. It is sad and cruel, that I know the truth, yet know no way to speak it. [*He turns to the figure of* ARTEMIS] Goddess, daughter of Leto, most dear companion, and comrade in the hunt, I shall live exiled for ever from glorious Athens! Farewell, my city; farewell, land of Erechtheus; farewell, plain of Troezen, rich in the vigorous delights of youth! I take my last look now, speak my last word to you. And you too, lads that have grown up with me here – come, say good-bye to me and see me to the border. Though even my own father denies it, you will never meet a man more honourable.

Exit HIPPOLYTUS with his men

CHORUS

> When I remember that the gods take thought
> For human life, often in hours of grief
>> To me this faith has brought
>> Comfort and heart's relief.

> Yet, though deep in my hope perception lies
> Wistful, experience grows and faith recedes:
>> Men's fortunes fall and rise
>> Not answering to their deeds.

Change follows change; Fate purposeless and blind
Uproots us from familiar soil:
    The longest life can find
    No rest from travel and toil.

This is my prayer: may divine providence fulfil
    All my heart's will,
    And bless my days with wealth, and guard
My life from pain, and keep my soul unscarred.

The dauntless stern resolve is not for me,
Nor the fair face masking the false intent;
    Rather my choice would be
To change my ways, adapt my easy creed
    To suit to-morrow's need,
And pass my quiet days in long content.

I cannot think clearly now:
I have seen a thing that I never thought to see –
I have seen the brightest star of the city of Athens
Driven out by his father's anger
To look for another country.
Sandy shore fringing the city-wall,
You will not see him now;
Nor you, oak-forests of the mountain-side,
Where in the train of the immortal Huntress
He followed with swift-footed hounds to make his kill!

We shall not see him now
Leap up behind his trained Thessalian team,
Holding the smooth track round the shore-marshes
Breathless with the tense drumming of hooves.
The music that sang unsleeping from the plucked string
Shall be dumb in his father's palace
The garlands will wither now

That you strewed in the deep Spring grass
Where Artemis loved to rest;
And the jealous war of girls who longed for your love,
Now you are gone, sinks into hopeless peace.

To me, Hippolytus, your fate has left
A life unreal, empty of all but tears.
   Dead are the dreams that lit
   Your mother's pains with joy.
Gods immortal, mortal rage reproaches you!
   How, you sister Graces,
Can you see him hounded from his father's home,
   Innocent, and outcast –
   Righteous, and uprooted?

CHORUS
Look! Someone is running this way! It is one of Hippolytus' men!
And his eyes are full of horror!

Enter MESSENGER

MESSENGER
Women, where can I find the King? Where is Theseus? If you
know, tell me. Is he indoors?

CHORUS
Here is the King. He is coming out now.

Enter THESEUS

MESSENGER
Theseus, I bring grave news – grave both for you and for all your
people, whether of Athens or of Troezen.

THESEUS
What is your news? Can yet another calamity have fallen upon
our two cities?

MESSENGER

Hippolytus is dead – or dying. His life hangs in the balance.

THESEUS

Who struck him? Was it the vengeance of some man whose wife
he had dishonoured as he did his father's?

MESSENGER

It was his own chariot that killed him – and the curses which your
lips called down from your father the sea-god upon your son.

THESEUS

By the gods! – so you have proved a true father to me, Poseidon:
you heard my curse! And how did it happen? Tell me! How did the
trap of justice close on the man who shamed me?

MESSENGER

We were on the shore, near the water's edge, combing down the
horses and smoothing their manes; and we were weeping, for we
had been told that Hippolytus was no longer free to come and go
in Troezen, but was condemned by you to the miseries of exile.
He came to us there, bringing the same tale of tears; and a great
troop of friends and followers, young men like himself, came with
him. After some time he stopped weeping and said to us, 'This is
folly; my father must be obeyed. Men, yoke my horses, harness
them to the chariot. This is not my country any more.' Then every
man of us came with a will, and sooner than you could say it we
had the team harnessed and standing ready at the prince's side.
He caught up the reins from the driving-rail, and, dressed as he
was for hunting, took his stand on the chariot. And first he held
up his hands and prayed: 'Zeus, may I die if I am a guilty man!
And may my father know how he has wronged me – if not while
I live, then after I am dead!'

And now he had gripped the goad and was urging his horses;
and we servants began running beside the bridles, to escort our

master along the straight road to Argos and Epidauria. We sped on, across the Troezenian frontier, and reached a deserted part of the coast, beyond which, as you know, a beach runs down to the Saronic Sea. It was there that we heard a heavy rumbling sound, like the thunder of Zeus, but rising out of the earth, with a deep roar that was horrible to hear. The horses pricked their ears, lifted their heads. We youths were terrified, wondering where the sound came from. We looked out to the breaking surf, and there we saw a wave of unearthly size, rearing to the sky; it hid from my view not only the Scironian headland but the Isthmus and the Rock of Asclepius. Then, swelling still huger, and spattering foam on every side, it rushed seething and hissing to the shore, and straight towards the chariot and the four horses. And in the very moment of bursting and crashing, the wave threw forth a monstrous savage bull, whose bellow filled the whole earth with an appalling echo, while the sight of him was too tremendous for mortal vision. The horses were seized with a frenzy of terror. Hippolytus, long versed in the ways of horses, gripped the reins, twisting them round behind his back and dragging on them as a rower tugs on his oar. It was no use: the beasts took the wrought-iron bits between their teeth and careered on, as though the driver's hand and the reins and harness and the heavy chariot were nothing at all! When he struggled to steer their hurtling course up towards the soft grass, there was the bull in front to craze them with terror and turn them back; when they went madly tearing towards the rocks, then the bull kept close beside them, silent, and swerving right in upon the chariot, until the moment when he crashed the boss of the wheel against a rock and flung the chariot tossing in the air. Then there was wild confusion – wheels, axle, bolts, and frame leaping high. Hippolytus, tangled in the reins, strung fast in an inextricable knot, was dragged along, his head dashed on the rocks, his flesh torn; while in a voice terrible to hear he shouted to his horses, 'Stop! You were reared in my own stables – will you grind me to death?' Then he cried, 'Father, why did you curse me? I am innocent! Will no one come to help me?'

Indeed, there were many of us willing enough, but run as we might we were left behind. At last – how I do not know – he fell clear of those fine reins that bound him. He still breathed; though there was little life left in him. The horses had vanished away over the rocky ground, I cannot tell where; so had that dreadful prodigy of a bull.

My lord: I am only one of your palace slaves; but I never can nor will believe that your son was guilty of so terrible a crime – no, not if the whole race of women hanged themselves, not if a mountain of letters were written to accuse him: I know that Hippolytus is a good man.

CHORUS
The wheel has turned; disaster follows disaster. Fate is inevitable; there is no escape.

THESEUS
Because I hated the man who has suffered this, I was glad when I heard it; but remembrance of the gods awes me: Hippolytus is my own flesh. What has happened gives me neither pleasure nor grief.

MESSENGER
What shall we do? Shall we bring him to die here? Or what would please you? Consider: your son is struck down. Listen to my advice and do not be harsh to him.

THESEUS
Bring him. Let me see face to face the man who denies that he dishonoured my bed; so that my words and the hand of heaven may convict him.

Exit MESSENGER

CHORUS
Aphrodite! You lead captive
Stubborn hearts of gods and mortals!

At your side with glinting wing
Eros, round his victim swiftly circling,
Hovers over earth and the salt sea's clear song.
When on the maddened spirit
He swoops with sweet enchantment,
Whelps of the mountain know the power of his golden wing;
Fish, and the unnumbered beasts that draw
Life from the earth's breast, warmth from the sun's eye –
Yes, and the hearts of men,
Yield to the universal spell.
Aphrodite, you alone
Reign in power and honour,
Queen of all creation!

THESEUS *and the* CHORUS *are facing the statue of* APHRODITE;
ARTEMIS *appears beside her own statue on the other side of the*
stage. As she speaks all turn towards her.

ARTEMIS
Theseus, royal son of Aegeus! I command you,
Listen! It is Artemis, Leto's daughter, who speaks.
Why do you, wretch, rejoice at what you have heard?
You have most sinfully murdered your own son.
You believed your wife's lies without witness: now
Witness the world how you reap your own undoing!
Will you not cower shamed in the depths of hell?
Soar to the sky to escape this chain of misery?
    In the common life of good men
    There is no place for you now.   [*She moves to centre of stage*]
    I will tell you, Theseus, the true state of your unhappy life; and
my words will not smooth your path, but sharpen your pain.
My purpose in coming is to disclose, first, your son's uprightness
of heart, that he may die with a good name; then, your wife's
frenzy – or, in some sense, her nobleness. Phaedra, plagued and
goaded by that goddess whom I, and all who love virginity, most

hate – Phaedra loved your son. Reason struggled to subdue passion. She died through schemes plotted against her will: her nurse told Hippolytus, under oath of secrecy, the Queen's affliction. He honourably resisted her persuasions; even when you so wronged him, still for reverence of the gods he would not abjure his oath; but Phaedra, in terror lest she be exposed, wrote that lying letter and by fraud killed your son – yes, for you believed her!

THESEUS
My son, my son!

ARTEMIS
Do my words hurt, Theseus? Listen further, for you have more to suffer. You know that your father promised you the fulfilment of three curses? The first you have most wickedly misused, cursing your son when you might have cursed an enemy. Your father the sea-god gave all that he was bound to give. He had promised; and the folly was not his. Now in his eyes and in mine you are condemned. Instead of waiting for proof, or prophetic guidance, giving no room for question or the slow scrutiny of Time, with unrighteous haste you flung your curse and killed your son.

THESEUS
Goddess, let me die!

ARTEMIS
Your sin is great. Yet even you may still find pardon for what you have done. For it was Aphrodite who, to satisfy her resentment, willed that all this should happen; and there is a law among gods, that no one of us should seek to frustrate another's purpose, but let well alone. I tell you, but that I fear Zeus and his laws, I never would have submitted to such dishonour, as to stand by and see Hippolytus go to his death; for he was dearest to me of all mortals. You did not know the truth: this, first, frees your fault from the

deepest guilt. Then, your wife by her death prevented any test of what she alleged, and thus made sure that you would believe her. So this flood of misfortune has burst chiefly upon you; but I too suffer. For a good man's death is no joy to the gods; but the impious man we utterly destroy, and his house and children with him.

CHORUS
Ah, look! Here comes the piteous prince,
His young flesh torn, his fair head bruised.
Ah, suffering house! The hand of heaven has struck
Twice in one day, accomplishing
The heavy doom of your appointed pain.

Enter HIPPOLYTUS, *supported by Huntsmen*

HIPPOLYTUS
Weep for me, weep for me,
Scarred, broken, trampled under foot
By man and god alike unjust –
My father's curse, Poseidon's power;
Weep for my death!
My forehead is pierced with the fierce pain,
My brain convulsed with the pulse of anguish.
Enough now! I am fainting; let me lie.   [*They lay him down*]
O horses my own hand fed,
Your cursed strength has crushed the breath from my body,
Torn the life from my limbs!
Men, for God's sake have careful hands
And touch me gently where the flesh is raw.
Who stands at my right side?
Lift me softly, with a steady grip.
Fallen cursed by my father's fault –
Zeus, do you see my agony?
I, that revered the gods with a holy heart,

I that was first in innocence,
Tread my way from life to the dark world,
And Death's eyes meet me as I go.

In vain I strove with patience
To love and serve my neighbour:
Now pain sets painful foot upon my body.
Let go, hold me no longer,
But let Death come to heal me;
And, if you pity me, help me to die quickly!
I am in love with the rending spear: come, cruel edge,
Shatter my heart and lull my life asleep!
Now, through my father's fatal curse,
The hellish heritage of bloodguiltiness
Won by forgotten ancestors
Descends impatient to the appointed heir –
On me it falls! Why? Why? I have done no wrong!
What shall I say? How can I ease my soul
And reach the end of anguish?
   Lay me deep for evermore,
   Death, with sore unyielding hand,
   In the land of night and sleep!

ARTEMIS
Poor soul, galled with a bitter yoke! It was your noble heart that
destroyed you.

HIPPOLYTUS
Ah, breath of divine fragrance! Goddess, I hear you, and my
torment lightens. Is it truly Artemis, here in this place?

ARTEMIS
Poor soul, it is. You have no better friend among the gods.

HIPPOLYTUS
Lady, you see how it is with me?

ARTEMIS
I see; but my eyes are forbidden to shed tears.

HIPPOLYTUS
No one now to attend you in the hunt. . . .

ARTEMIS
No: you were my dear attendant; and you are dying.

HIPPOLYTUS
None to graze your horses, or guard your statues.

ARTEMIS
The wicked craft of Aphrodite has done this.

HIPPOLYTUS
Aphrodite! So, I know what god has killed me.

ARTEMIS
She resented your neglect and hated your purity.

HIPPOLYTUS
It is clear to me now: she has destroyed us all three.

ARTEMIS
You, and your father, and your father's wife.

HIPPOLYTUS
Though my father wronged me, yet I weep for him.

ARTEMIS
He was deceived: a god had planned it so.

HIPPOLYTUS
Father, how you have suffered to-day!

THESEUS
My son, my heart is broken; life is loathsome to me.

HIPPOLYTUS
Though the fault was yours, I weep for you more than for myself.

THESEUS
Would God I might die for you, my son!

HIPPOLYTUS
You too had little joy of your father's gifts.

THESEUS
O that that curse had never passed my lips!

HIPPOLYTUS
Why? You would have killed me, you were so angry then!

THESEUS
I was cheated by the gods out of my right mind!

HIPPOLYTUS
Oh, if only a man's curse could touch a god!

ARTEMIS
You need not curse. Not even the black depths
Beneath the earth shall thwart the vengeance due
For this cruel wrong that Aphrodite's rage
Wreaked on your body for your pure soul's sake.
I will requite her: with this unfailing bow
My own hand shall strike down in just return
The man her heart holds dearest in the world.

   On you, poor youth, I will bestow a place
Of highest honour in the city of Troezen.
The unmarried virgins shall, before their marriage,

Cut off their hair for you; age after age
Harvest of tears and mourning shall be yours,
Music of maidens' sorrow for your death.
And Phaedra too shall give her name to memory,
And songs shall celebrate her love for you.

    Theseus, remember your own father Aegeus:
Embrace your son and clasp him to your heart.
His death was not your will: men may well sin,
When the gods so ordain.
                  Hippolytus,
You must not hate your father; you know now
The destiny which has destroyed your life.
Farewell: I may not look upon the dead,
Nor stain my sight with death's last agony;
And now I see that you are near your end.

HIPPOLYTUS
Farewell, immortal Virgin! Easy it is
For you to sever our long fellowship.
Since you desire it, I forgive my father,
As in days past I have obeyed your word.
Ah!
Darkness is closing now over my eyes.
Father, take hold of me; lift me upright.

THESEUS
What is it, dear son? Will you break my heart?

HIPPOLYTUS
I stand before Death's gates; I see them open.

THESEUS
And will you leave me guilty and defiled?

HIPPOLYTUS
No, no! I here absolve you of my death!

THESEUS
What? You will free me from the stain of blood?

HIPPOLYTUS
I swear it by the conquering bow of Artemis.

THESEUS
Dear son, how noble a heart you show your father!

HIPPOLYTUS
Pray that your true-born sons may be like me!

THESEUS
O generous soul, dying in innocence!

HIPPOLYTUS
Farewell, my Father! Farewell, and farewell!

THESEUS
Do not forsake me now! Courage, my son!

HIPPOLYTUS
My time for courage is past. I am gone, Father.
Cover my face now quickly with my cloak. [*He dies*]

THESEUS
      Land of Athens, frontiers of a famous city!
        When was man more noble?
        When was loss more bitter?
     Aphrodite! with what endless tears and anguish
        Shall your cruel contriving
        Haunt my heart for ever!

CHORUS

> Grief unlooked-for now fills every heart alike;
>> Tears from all eyes falling
>> Shall make mournful music.
> He was noble: loudly then from every tongue
>> Praise and lamentation
>> Through the world shall echo!

THE BACCHAE

CHARACTERS

DIONYSUS

CHORUS *of Oriental women, devotees of Dionysus*

TEIRESIAS *a blind Seer*

CADMUS *founder of Thebes, and formerly king*

PENTHEUS *his grandson, now king of Thebes*

A GUARD *attending Pentheus*

A HERDSMAN

A MESSENGER

AGAUË *daughter of Cadmus and mother of Pentheus*

◳

THE BACCHAE

Scene: Before the palace of Pentheus in Thebes. At one side of the stage is the monument of Semele; above it burns a low flame, and around it are the remains of ruined and blackened masonry.

DIONYSUS *enters on stage right. He has a crown of ivy, a thyrsus in his hand, and a fawnskin draped over his body. He has long flowing hair and a youthful, almost feminine beauty.*

DIONYSUS

I am Dionysus, son of Zeus. My mother was Semele, daughter of Cadmus; I was delivered from her womb by the fire of a lightning-flash. To-day I have laid aside the appearance of a god, and have come disguised as a mortal man to this city of Thebes, where flow the two rivers, Dirce and Ismenus. Here by the palace I see the monument recording my mother's death by lightning; here are the smouldering ruins of her house, which bear the still living flame of Zeus's fire – the undying token of Hera's cruelty to my mother. Cadmus does well to keep this ground untrodden, a precinct consecrated to his daughter; and I now have decked it round with sprays of young vine-leaves.

My home is in the lands of Lydia and Phrygia, fertile in gold. From there I visited the sun-beaten Persian plains, the walled towns of Bactria, harsh Media, wealthy Arabia, and the whole of that Asian sea-board where Greeks and Orientals live side by side in crowded magnificent cities; and before reaching this, the first city of Hellas I have seen, I had already, in all those regions of the East, danced my dance and established my ritual, to make my godhead manifest to mortal men.

117

And the reason why Thebes is the first place in Hellas where, at my command, women have raised the Bacchic shout, put on the fawnskin cloak, and taken in their hands my weapon, the thyrsus wreathed with ivy – the reason is this: my mother's sisters said – what they should have been the last to say – that I, Dionysus, was not the progeny of Zeus; but that Semele, being with child by some mortal, at her father's suggestion ascribed to Zeus the loss of her virginity; and they loudly insisted that this lie about the father-hood of her child was the sin for which Zeus had struck her dead.

Therefore I have plagued these same sisters with madness, and driven them all frantic out of doors; now their home is the moun-tains, and their wits are gone. And I made them carry the emblems of my mysteries; and the whole female population of Thebes, every woman there was in the town, I drove raving from their homes; now they have joined the daughters of Cadmus, and there they are, sitting roofless on the rocks under the silver fir-trees. Thebes must learn, unwilling though she is, that my Bacchic revels are something beyond her present knowledge and understanding; and I must vindicate the honour of my mother Semele, by mani-festing myself before the human race as the god whom she bore to Zeus.

Now Cadmus has handed over his kingly honours and his throne to his daughter's son Pentheus. And this Pentheus is a fighter against God – he defies me, excludes me from libations, never names me in prayer. Therefore I will demonstrate to him, and to all Thebes, that I am a god.

When I have set all in order here, I will pass on to some other place, and manifest myself. Meanwhile, if the Theban city in anger tries to bring the Bacchae home from the mountains by force, I will join that army of women possessed and lead them to battle. And this is why I have changed my divine form to human, and appear in the likeness of a man.

Come, my holy band of revellers, women I have brought from lands of the East, from the slopes of Tmolus, bastion of Lydia, to be with me and share my travels! Raise the music of your Phrygian

home, the timbrels invented by Rhea the Great Mother and by
me; surround the palace of Pentheus and strike up such a peal of
sound as shall make Thebes turn to look! I will go to the glens of
Cithaeron where my Bacchae are, and join their dances.

DIONYSUS *goes out towards the mountain; the* CHORUS *enter*
where DIONYSUS *entered, from the road by which they have*
travelled.

CHORUS
 From far-off lands of Asia,
 From Tmolus the holy mountain,
 We run with the god of laughter;
 Labour is joy and weariness is sweet,
 And our song resounds to Bacchus!

 Beware of the interloper!
 Indoors or out, who listens?
 Let every lip be holy;
 Stand well aloof, be silent, while we sing
 The appointed hymn to Bacchus!

 Blest is the happy man
 Who knows the mysteries the gods ordain,
 And sanctifies his life,
 Joins soul with soul in mystic unity,
 And, by due ritual made pure,
 Enters the ecstasy of mountain solitudes;
 Who observes the mystic rites
 Made lawful by Cybele the Great Mother;
 Who crowns his head with ivy,
 And shakes aloft his wand in worship of Dionysus.

 On, on! Run, dance, delirious, possessed!
 Dionysus comes to his own;

Bring from the Phrygian hills to the broad streets of Hellas
The god, child of a god,
Spirit of revel and rapture, Dionysus!

Once, on the womb that held him
The fire-bolt flew from the hand of Zeus;
And pains of child-birth bound his mother fast,
And she cast him forth untimely,
And under the lightning's lash relinquished life;
And Zeus the son of Cronos
Ensconced him instantly in a secret womb
Chambered within his thigh,
And with golden pins closed him from Hera's sight.

So, when the Fates had made him ripe for birth,
Zeus bore the bull-horned god
And wreathed his head with wreaths of writhing snakes;
Which is why the Maenads catch
Wild snakes, nurse them and twine them round their hair.

O Thebes, old nurse that cradled Semele,
Be ivy-garlanded, burst into flower
With wreaths of lush bright-berried bryony,
Bring sprays of fir, green branches torn from oaks,
Fill soul and flesh with Bacchus' mystic power;
Fringe and bedeck your dappled fawnskin cloaks
With woolly tufts and locks of purest white.
There's a brute wildness in the fennel-wands –
Reverence it well. Soon the whole land will dance
    When the god with ecstatic shout
    Leads his companies out
    To the mountain's mounting height
    Swarming with riotous bands
    Of Theban women leaving
    Their spinning and their weaving

Stung with the maddening trance
   Of Dionysus!

O secret chamber the Curetes knew!
O holy cavern in the Cretan glade
Where Zeus was cradled, where for our delight
The triple-crested Corybantes drew
Tight the round drum-skin, till its wild beat made
Rapturous rhythm to the breathing sweetness
Of Phrygian flutes! Then divine Rhea found
The drum could give her Bacchic airs completeness;
   From her, the Mother of all,
   The crazy Satyrs soon,
   In their dancing festival
   When the second year comes round,
   Seized on the timbrel's tune
   To play the leading part
   In feasts that delight the heart
     Of Dionysus.

O what delight is in the mountains!
There the celebrant, wrapped in his sacred fawnskin,
Flings himself on the ground surrendered,
While the swift-footed company streams on;
There he hunts for blood, and rapturously
Eats the raw flesh of the slaughtered goat,
Hurrying on to the Phrygian or Lydian mountain heights.
Possessed, ecstatic, he leads their happy cries;
The earth flows with milk, flows with wine,
Flows with nectar of bees;
The air is thick with a scent of Syrian myrrh.
The celebrant runs entranced, whirling the torch
That blazes red from the fennel-wand in his grasp,
And with shouts he rouses the scattered bands,
Sets their feet dancing,

As he shakes his delicate locks to the wild wind.
And amidst the frenzy of song he shouts like thunder:
'On, on! Run, dance, delirious, possessed!
You, the beauty and grace of golden Tmolus,
Sing to the rattle of thunderous drums,
Sing for joy,
Praise Dionysus, god of joy!
Shout like Phrygians, sing out the tunes you know,
While the sacred pure-toned flute
Vibrates the air with holy merriment,
In time with the pulse of the feet that flock
To the mountains, to the mountains!'
And, like a foal with its mother at pasture,
Runs and leaps for joy every daughter of Bacchus.

Enter TEIRESIAS. *Though blind, he makes his way*
unaided to the door, and knocks

TEIRESIAS

Who keeps the gate? [*A servant is heard answering from inside*]
Call out Cadmus, the son of Agenor, who came from Sidonia to
build these walls of Thebes. Go, someone, tell him Teiresias is
looking for him. He knows why I have come – the agreement I
made with him – old as I am, and he older still – to get myself a
Bacchic wand, put on the fawnskin cloak, and wear a garland of
young ivy-shoots.

Enter CADMUS

CADMUS

O my dear friend, I knew your voice, although I was indoors, as
soon as I heard it – the wise voice of a wise man. Look, I am ready,
I have everything the god prescribes. Dionysus is my own
daughter's son; and now he has shown himself to the world as a
god, it is right that I should do all I can to exalt him. Where
should we go to dance, and take our stand with the rest, tossing

our old grey beards? You must guide me in this, Teiresias –
you're nearly as old as I am, and you understand such matters. No,
it won't be too much for me; I can beat time with my thyrsus night
and day! It's a happy thing to forget one's age.

TEIRESIAS

Then you feel just as I do. I am young too; I'll make an attempt
at the dance.

CADMUS

You don't think we should make our way to the mountains in a
carriage?

TEIRESIAS

No, no, that would not show the same respect for the god.

CADMUS

I'll be your guide then – two old men together.

TEIRESIAS

The god will guide us there, and without weariness.

CADMUS

Shall we be the only men in Thebes who dance to Bacchus?

TEIRESIAS

We are the only men right-minded; the rest are perverse.

CADMUS

We are wasting time. Now, take my hand.

TEIRESIAS

There; hold firmly, with a good grip.

CADMUS

Mortals must not make light of the gods – *I* would never do so.

TEIRESIAS

We entertain no theories or speculations in divine matters. The beliefs we have received from our ancestors – beliefs as old as time – cannot be destroyed by any argument, nor by any ingenuity the mind can invent. No doubt I shall be criticized for wearing an ivy-wreath and setting off for the dance; they will say I have no sense of what befits my age. They will be wrong: the god has drawn no distinction between young and old, which should dance and which should not. He wishes to receive honour alike from all; he will not have his worship made a matter of nice calculation.

CADMUS

Teiresias, since you are blind I must be your prophet. I see Pentheus the son of Echion, to whom I have resigned my rule in Thebes, hurrying towards the palace. He looks thoroughly upset! What is he going to tell us?

Enter PENTHEUS. *He addresses the audience, without at first noticing* CADMUS *and* TEIRESIAS, *who stand at the opposite side of the stage.*

PENTHEUS

I've been away from Thebes, as it happens; but I've heard the news – this extraordinary scandal in the city. Our women, I discover, have abandoned their homes on some pretence of Bacchic worship, and go gadding about in the woods on the mountain-side, dancing in honour of this upstart god Dionysus, whoever he may be. They tell me, in the midst of each group of revellers stands a bowl full of wine; and the women go creeping off this way and that to lonely places and there give themselves to lecherous men, under the excuse that they are Maenad priestesses; though in their ritual Aphrodite comes before Bacchus.

Well, those that I've caught, my guards are keeping safe; we've tied their hands, and lodged them at state expense. Those still at large on the mountain I am going to hunt out; and that includes my own mother Agauë, and her sisters Ino and Autonoë. Once I have them secure in iron chains I shall soon put a stop to this outrageous Bacchism.

I understand too that some Oriental magician or conjurer has arrived from Lydia, a fellow with golden hair flowing in scented ringlets, the flush of wine in his face and the charm of Aphrodite in his eyes; and that he entices our young girls with his Bacchic mysteries, and spends day and night in their company. Only let me get that fellow inside my walls – I'll cut his head from his shoulders; that will finish his thyrsus-waving and hair-tossing. *He* is the one – this foreigner – who has spread stories about Dionysus, that he is a god, that he was sewn up in Zeus's thigh. The truth about Dionysus is that he's dead, burnt to a cinder by lightning along with his mother, because of her lying story that Zeus had come to her bed. But whoever this man may be, does not his insufferable behaviour merit the worst of punishments, hanging?

He turns to go, and sees CADMUS *and* TEIRESIAS

Why, look! Another miracle! Here's the prophet Teiresias, and my mother's father, playing the Bacchant, in dappled fawnskin and carrying fennel-wands! Well, there's a sight for laughter! [*But he is raging, not laughing*] Sir, I am ashamed to see two men of your age with so little sense of decency. Come, you are my grand-father: throw away your garland, get rid of that thyrsus. *You* persuaded him into this, Teiresias. No doubt you hope that, when you have introduced this new god to the people, you will be his appointed seer, you will collect the fees for sacrifices. Your grey hairs are your protection; otherwise you should sit with all these crazy females in prison, for encouraging such pernicious performances.

As for women, my opinion is this: when the sparkle of sweet wine appears at their feasts, no good can be expected from their ceremonies.

CHORUS

What profanity! Sir, do you not revere the gods, or Cadmus, who sowed the seed of the earth-born men? Echion your father was one of them – will you shame your own blood?

TEIRESIAS

When a clever man has a plausible theme to argue, to be eloquent is no great feat. But though you seem, by your glib tongue, to be intelligent, yet your words are foolish. Power and eloquence in a headstrong man can only lead to folly; and such a man is a danger to the state.

This new divinity whom you ridicule – no words of mine could adequately express the ascendancy he is destined to achieve through the length and breadth of Hellas. There are two powers, young man, which are supreme in human affairs: first, the goddess Demeter; she is the Earth – call her by what name you will; and she supplies mankind with solid food. Second, Dionysus the son of Semele; the blessing he provides is the counterpart to the blessing of bread; he discovered and bestowed on men the service of drink, the juice that streams from the vine-clusters; men have but to take their fill of wine, and the sufferings of an unhappy race are banished, each day's troubles are forgotten in sleep – indeed this is our only cure for the weariness of life. Dionysus, himself a god, is poured out in offering to the gods; so that through him mankind receives blessing.

Now for the legend that he was sewn up in Zeus's thigh – do you mock at it? Then I will explain to you the truth that lies in the legend. When Zeus snatched the infant Dionysus away from the fire of the lightning, and brought him to Olympus as a god, Hera wanted to cast him out of heaven; so, to prevent her, Zeus – as you would expect – devised a plan. He broke off a piece of the sky that envelops the earth, made it into the likeness of a child, and gave it to Hera as a pledge, to soothe her jealousy. He entrusted the true Dionysus to others to bring up. Now the ancient word for a *pledge* is very similar to our word 'thigh'; and so in time the word was mistaken, and men said Dionysus was saved by Zeus's *thigh*, instead of by Zeus's *pledge*, because a pledge was given to Hera in his likeness.

And this god is a prophet; for the Bacchic ecstasy and frenzy contain a strong element of prophecy. When Dionysus enters in power into a human body, he endows the possessed person with power to foretell the future. He also in some degree shares the function of Ares, god of war. It has happened that an army, equipped and stationed for battle, has fled in panic before a spear has been raised. This too is a madness sent by Dionysus.

Ay, and the day will come when you shall see him on the very rocks of Delphi, amidst flaring torches bounding over the twin-peaked ridge, hurling and brandishing his Bacchic staff, honoured by all Hellas.

Come, Pentheus, listen to me. You rely on force; but it is not force that governs human affairs. If you think otherwise – beware of mistaking your perverse opinion for wisdom. Welcome Dionysus to Thebes; pour libations to him, garland your head and celebrate his rites. Dionysus will not compel women to control their lusts. Self-control in all things depends on our own natures. This is a fact you should consider; for a chaste-minded woman will come to no harm in the rites of Bacchus. And think of this too: when crowds stand at the city gates, and the people glorify the name of Pentheus, you are filled with pleasure; so, I think, Dionysus is glad to receive honour.

So then I, and Cadmus, whom you mock, will wear the ivy-wreath and join in the dancing – we are both old men, but this is our duty; and no words of yours shall persuade me to fight against the gods. For your mind is most pitifully diseased; and just as your disease springs from incantations, so there is no incantation that can cure you.

CHORUS
What you have said, Teiresias, means no dishonour to Phoebus,

whose prophet you are; and shows your wisdom in honouring
Dionysus as a great god.

CADMUS

My son, Teiresias has advised you well. Do not venture outside the
customary pieties; stay with us. Just now your wits are scattered;
you think you are talking sense, but it is not sense at all. And even
if you are right, and this god is not a god, at least let him have your
word of acknowledgment; lie for a good purpose, so that Semele
may be honoured as mother of a god, and I and our whole family
may gain in dignity. Remember Actaeon – his tragic end; he
boasted, out in these valleys, that he was a better hunter than
Artemis, and was torn to pieces and devoured by the very hounds
he had bred. Don't invite the same fate! Come, let me put this
ivy-wreath on your head. Join us in worshipping Dionysus.

PENTHEUS

Keep your hands off! Go to your Bacchic rites; and don't wipe off
your crazy folly on me! But I will punish this man who has taught
you your lunacy. Go, one of you, immediately to the place of
augury where Teiresias practises, smash it with crowbars, knock
down the walls, turn everything upside down, fling out his holy
fripperies to the winds. That will sting him more than anything
else. The rest of you, comb the city and find this effeminate
foreigner, who plagues our women with this strange disease and
turns them into whores. If you catch him, bring him here in chains,
and I'll have him stoned to death. He shall be sorry he ever came
revelling in Thebes.

Exit PENTHEUS

TEIRESIAS

Foolhardy man, you don't know what you are saying. You were
out of your mind before; now you are raving mad.

Come, Cadmus; let us go and pray both for this man, brutish
as he is, and for Thebes, and entreat Dionysus to be forbearing.

Come, take your thyrsus and follow. Try to support me – there, we will help each other. It would be a pity for us both to fall; but never mind that. We must pay our service to Dionysus the son of Zeus.

Cadmus, the name *Pentheus* means *grief*. Let us hope he is not going to bring grief on your house. I am not speaking by inspiration; I judge by his conduct. The things he has said reveal the depth of his folly.

Exeunt TEIRESIAS *and* CADMUS

CHORUS
    Holiness, Queen of heaven,
    Holiness, golden-winged ranging the earth,
    Do you hear his blasphemy?
    Pentheus dares – do you hear? – to revile the god of joy,
    The son of Semele, who when the gay-crowned feast is set
    Is named among gods the chief;
    Whose gifts are joy and union of soul in dancing,
    Joy in music of flutes,
    Joy when sparkling wine at feasts of the gods
    Soothes the sore regret,
    Banishes every grief,
    When the reveller rests, enfolded deep
    In the cool shade of ivy-shoots,
    On wine's soft pillow of sleep.

    The brash, unbridled tongue,
    The lawless folly of fools, will end in pain.
    But the life of wise content
    Is blest with quietness, escapes the storm
    And keeps its house secure.
    Though blessed gods dwell in the distant skies,
    They watch the ways of men.
    To know much is not to be wise.
    Pride more than mortal hastens life to its end;

And they who in pride pretend
Beyond man's limit, will lose what lay
Close to their hand and sure.
I count it madness, and know no cure can mend
The evil man and his evil way.

O to set foot on Aphrodite's island,
On Cyprus, haunted by the Loves, who enchant
Brief life with sweetness; or in that strange land
Whose fertile river carves a hundred channels
To enrich her rainless sand;
Or where the sacred pastures of Olympus slant
Down to Pieria, where the Muses dwell –
Take me, O Bromius, take me and inspire
Laughter and worship! There our holy spell
And ecstasy are welcome; there the gentle band
Of Graces have their home, and sweet Desire.

Dionysus, son of Zeus, delights in banquets;
And his dear love is Peace, giver of wealth,
Saviour of young men's lives – a goddess rare!
In wine, his gift that charms all griefs away,
Alike both rich and poor may have their part.
His enemy is the man who has no care
To pass his years in happiness and health,
His days in quiet and his nights in joy,
Watchful to keep aloof both mind and heart
From men whose pride claims more than mortals may.
The life that wins the poor man's common voice,
His creed, his practice – this shall be my choice.

Some of the guards whom PENTHEUS *sent to arrest* DIONYSUS
now enter with their prisoner. PENTHEUS *enters from the palace*

GUARD
Well, sir, we went after this lion you told us to hunt, and we have

been successful. But – we found the lion was tame! He made no attempt to escape, but freely held out his hands to be bound. He didn't even turn pale, but kept the fresh colour you see in his face now, smiling, and telling us to tie him up and run him in; waited for me, in fact – gave us no trouble at all. Naturally I felt a bit awkward. 'You'll excuse me, sir,' I said, 'I don't want to arrest you, but it's the king's orders.'

And there's another thing, sir. Those women you rounded up and put in fetters and in prison, those religious maniacs – why, they're all gone, let loose to the glens; and there they are, dancing and calling on Bacchus. The fetters simply fell from their limbs, the bolts flew back without the touch of any mortal hand, and let the doors open. Master, this man has come to our city of Thebes with a load of miracles. What is going to happen next is your concern, not mine.

PENTHEUS
Untie his hands. [*The guard does so*] He is in the trap, and he's not nimble enough to escape me now.

Well, my man: you have a not unhandsome figure – for attracting women, which is your object in coming to Thebes. Those long curls of yours show that you're no wrestler – cascading close over your cheeks, most seductively. Your complexion, too, shows a carefully-preserved whiteness; you keep out of the sun and walk in the shade, to use your lovely face for courting Aphrodite. . . .

Ah, well; tell me first what country you were born in.

DIONYSUS
That is easily told without boasting. Doubtless you have heard of the flowery mountain, Tmolus.

PENTHEUS
Yes, the range that curves round the city of Sardis.

DIONYSUS
That was my home; I am a Lydian.

PENTHEUS
And why do you bring these rituals to Hellas?

DIONYSUS
Dionysus the son of Zeus instructed me.

PENTHEUS
Is there a Lydian Zeus, then, who begets new gods?

DIONYSUS
No; I speak of your Zeus, who made Semele his bride here in Thebes.

PENTHEUS
And when Dionysus took possession of you, did he appear in a dream by night, or visible before your eyes?

DIONYSUS
I saw him face to face; and he entrusted to me these mysteries.

PENTHEUS
What form do these mysteries of yours take?

DIONYSUS
That cannot be told to the uninitiated.

PENTHEUS
What do the worshippers gain from it?

DIONYSUS
That is not lawful for you to hear – yet it is worth hearing.

PENTHEUS
A clever answer, baited to rouse my curiosity.

DIONYSUS
Curiosity will be useless; the rites of the god abhor an impious
man.

PENTHEUS
If you say you saw Dionysus clearly – what was his appearance?

DIONYSUS
It was what he wished it to be. I had no say in that.

PENTHEUS
Another clever evasion, telling nothing.

DIONYSUS
A wise speech sleeps in a foolish ear.

PENTHEUS
Is this the first place where you have introduced Dionysus?

DIONYSUS
No; every Eastern land dances these mysteries.

PENTHEUS
I believe it. Oriental standards are altogether inferior to ours.

DIONYSUS
In this point they are superior. But their customs are different.

PENTHEUS
Do you celebrate your mysteries by night or by day?

DIONYSUS
Chiefly by night. Darkness induces religious awe.

PENTHEUS
For women darkness is treacherous and impure.

DIONYSUS
Impurity can be practised by daylight too.

PENTHEUS
It is time you were punished for your foul, slippery tongue.

DIONYSUS
And you for your crass impieties.

PENTHEUS
How bold his Bacchic inspiration makes him! He knows how to argue too.

DIONYSUS
Tell me my sentence. What punishment are you going to inflict?

PENTHEUS
First I'll cut off your scented silky hair.

DIONYSUS
My hair I keep for the god; it is sacred to him.

PENTHEUS
Next, hand over that thyrsus.

DIONYSUS
Take it from me yourself. I carry it for Dionysus, whose it is.

PENTHEUS
And I shall keep you safe in prison.

DIONYSUS
The god himself will set me free whenever I wish.

PENTHEUS
Set you free? When you stand among those frenzied women and
pray to him – no doubt!

DIONYSUS
He is here, close by me, and sees what is being done to me.

PENTHEUS
Oh, indeed? Where? To my eyes he is quite invisible.

DIONYSUS
Here at my side. You, being a blasphemer, cannot see him.

PENTHEUS [*to the guards*]
Get hold of him. He is laughing at me and the whole city.

DIONYSUS [*to the guards*]
I warn you not to bind me. . . . [*To* PENTHEUS] I am sane, you
are mad.

PENTHEUS [*to* DIONYSUS]
My orders overrule yours. [*To the guards*] Bind him, I tell you.

DIONYSUS
You do not know what life you live, or what you do, or who you
are.

PENTHEUS
Who I am? Pentheus, son of Echion and Agauë.

DIONYSUS
Pentheus means 'sorrow'. The name fits you well.

PENTHEUS

Take him away. Imprison him over there in the stables; he'll have
all the darkness he wants. – You can dance in there! As for these
women you've brought to aid and abet you, I shall either send them
to the slave market, or retain them in my own household to work
at the looms; that will keep their hands from drumming on
tambourines!

DIONYSUS

I will go. Nothing can happen to me that is not my destiny. But
Dionysus, who you say is dead, will pursue you and take his
revenge for this sacrilege. You are putting *him* in prison, when you
lay hands on me.

Guards take DIONYSUS *away to the stables; Pentheus follows*

CHORUS
   Dirce, sweet and holy maid,
   Acheloüs' Theban daughter,
   Once the child of Zeus was made
   Welcome in your welling water,
   When the lord of earth and sky
   Snatched him from the undying flame,
   Laid him safe within his thigh,
   Calling loud the infant's name:
   'Twice-born Dithyrambus! Come,
   Enter here your father's womb;
   Bacchic child, I now proclaim
   This in Thebes shall be your name.'
 Now, divine Dirce, when my head is crowned
 And my feet dance in Bacchus' revelry –
 Now you reject me from your holy ground.
 Why should you fear me? By the purple fruit
 That glows in glory on Dionysus' tree,
 His dread name yet shall haunt your memory!

O what anger lies beneath
Pentheus' voice and sullen face –
Offspring of the dragon's teeth,
And Echion's earth-born race,
Brute with bloody jaws agape,
God-defying, gross and grim,
Slander of his human shape!
Soon he'll chain us limb to limb –
Bacchus' servants! Yes, and more.
Even now our comrade lies
Deep on his dark prison floor.
Dionysus! do your eyes
See us? O son of Zeus, the oppressor's rod
Falls on your worshippers; come, mighty god,
Brandish your golden thyrsus and descend
From great Olympus; touch this murderous man,
And bring his violence to a sudden end!

Where are you, Dionysus? Leading your dancing bands
Over the mountain slopes, past many a wild beast's lair,
Or upon rocky crags, with the thyrsus in their hands?
Or in the wooded coverts, maybe, of Olympus, where
Orpheus once gathered the trees and mountain beasts,
Gathered them with his lyre, and sang an enchanting air.
Happy vale of Pieria! Bacchus delights in you;
He will cross the flood and foam of the Axius river, and there
He will bring his whirling Maenads, with dancing and with
    feasts –
Cross the father of waters, Lydias, generous giver
Of wealth and luck, they say, to the land he wanders through,
Whose famous horses graze by the rich and lovely river.

Suddenly a shout is heard from inside the building –
the voice of DIONYSUS

DIONYSUS

> Io, Io! Do you know my voice, do you hear?
> Worshippers of Bacchus! Io, Io!

CHORUS

Who is that? Where is he? The voice of Dionysus calling to us!

DIONYSUS

Io, Io! Hear me again: I am the son of Semele, the son of Zeus!

CHORUS

> Io, Io, our lord, our lord!
> Come, then, come to our company, lord of joy!

DIONYSUS

O dreadful earthquake, shake the floor of the world!

CHORUS [*with a scream of terror*]

Pentheus' palace is falling, crumbling in pieces!
[*They continue severally*]
Dionysus stands in the palace; bow before him!
We bow before him. See how the roof and pillars
Plunge to the ground! God from the inner prison
Will shout the shout of victory.

> *The flame on Semele's tomb grows and brightens*

DIONYSUS

Fan to a blaze the flame the lightning lit;
Kindle the conflagration of Pentheus' palace!

CHORUS

Look, look, look!
Do you see, do you see the flame of Semele's tomb,
The flame that remained when she died of the lightning-stroke?

A noise of crashing masonry is heard

Down, trembling Maenads! Hurl yourselves to the ground!
Your god is wrecking the palace, roof to floor;
He heard our cry – he is coming, the son of Zeus!

DIONYSUS *appears*

DIONYSUS
Women of Asia, why are you cowering terrified on the ground?
You heard Bacchus himself shattering Pentheus' palace; come,
stand up! Stop this trembling! Courage!

CHORUS
Oh, what a joy to hear your Bacchic shout! You have saved us.
We were deserted and alone: how happy we are to see you!

DIONYSUS
Were you plunged in despair, when I was sent inside to be thrown
into Pentheus' dark dungeon?

CHORUS
How could we help it? Who was there to protect us, if you were
taken? But tell us how you escaped from the clutches of this
wicked man.

DIONYSUS
I alone with effortless ease delivered myself.

CHORUS
But did he not bind your arms with knotted ropes?

DIONYSUS
Ha, ha! There I made a mockery of him. He thought he was
binding me; but he fed himself on delusion – he neither took hold

of me nor even touched me. Near the stall where he took me to shut me in, he found a bull; and he was tying his rope round the bull's knees and hooves, panting with rage, dripping sweat, and biting his lips; while I sat quietly by and watched him. And it was then that Bacchus came and shook the building and made the flame on his mother's tomb flare up. When Pentheus saw this, he imagined the place was on fire, and went rushing this way and that, calling to the servants to bring water, till the whole household was in commotion – all for nothing.

Then he thought I had escaped. He left throwing water, snatched up his murderous sword and darted into the palace. Thereupon Dionysus – or so it seemed to me; I tell what I thought – made a phantom figure appear in the palace court-yard; and Pentheus flew at it, and kept stabbing at the sunny air, imagining he was killing *me*.

But the god had further humiliation in store for him: he laid the stable-buildings in ruins on the ground – there they lie, a heap of rubble, to break his heart as he looks at my prison. Now he is helpless with exhaustion. He has dropped his sword. He, a mortal man, dared to take arms against a god. I walked quietly out of the palace, and here I am. Pentheus does not disturb me. But I hear his heavy tread indoors; I think he will be out here in a moment. What will he say after this? For all his rage, he shall not ruffle me. The wise man preserves a smooth-tempered self-control.

Enter PENTHEUS

PENTHEUS
This is outrageous. That foreigner was locked up and in chains a little while ago; now he has escaped me. [*He sees* DIONYSUS *and gives an excited shout*] That's the man! What's going on? How did you get out? How dare you show yourself here before my very doors?

DIONYSUS
Stay where you are. You are angry. Now control yourself.

PENTHEUS
You were bound and locked in: how did you escape?

DIONYSUS
Did you not hear me say that I should be set free by –

PENTHEUS
By whom? Everything you say is strange.

DIONYSUS
By him who plants for mortals the rich-clustered vine.

PENTHEUS
The god who makes men fools and women mad.

DIONYSUS
A splendid insult, that, to Dionysus!

PENTHEUS [*to attendant guards*]
Close the gates all round – every gate in the city wall.

DIONYSUS
And why? Cannot gods pass even over walls?

PENTHEUS
Oh, you know everything – except the things you ought to know.

DIONYSUS
The things one ought to know most of all, those things I know.
   But first listen to what this man has to tell you; he comes from
the mountains with news. – I will stay here; I promise not to run
away.

Enter a HERDSMAN

HERDSMAN

Pentheus, ruler of Thebes! I come from Cithaeron, where the ground is never free from dazzling shafts of snow.

PENTHEUS

And what urgent news do you bring me?

HERDSMAN

I have seen the holy Bacchae, who in madness went streaming bare-limbed out of the city gates. I have come with the intention of telling you, my lord, and the city, of their strange and terrible doings – things past all wonder. But I would like to know first if I may speak freely of what is going on there, or if I should trim my words. I am afraid of your hastiness, my lord, your hot temper; you are too much like a king.

PENTHEUS

Say all that you have to say; fear nothing from me. The more terrible your story about the Bacchae, the more certainly will I execute justice upon this man, the instigator of their wickedness.

HERDSMAN

Just when the sun's rays first beamed out to warm the earth, I was pasturing my cattle and working up towards the high ground; when I saw three groups of women who had been dancing together. The leader of one group was Autonoë; your mother Agaüe was at the head of the second, and Ino of the third. They were all sleeping, stretched out and quiet. Some rested on beds of pine-needles, some had pillows of oak-leaves; they lay just as they had thrown themselves down on the ground – but with modesty in their posture; they were not drunk with wine, as you told us, or with music of flutes; nor was there any love-making there in the loneliness of the woods.

As soon as your mother Agaüe heard the lowing of the horned cattle, she stood up among the Bacchae and called loudly to them to rouse themselves from sleep. And they threw off the strong sleep from their eyes and leapt to their feet. They were a sight to marvel at for modesty and comeliness – women old and young, and girls still unmarried. First they let down their hair over their shoulders; those whose fawnskins had come loose from their fastenings tied them up; and they girdled the dappled fur with snakes which licked their cheeks. And some would have in their arms a young gazelle, or wild wolf-cubs, and give them their own white milk – those who had infants at home recently born, so that their breasts were still full. And they wreathed their heads with garlands of ivy and oak and flowering bryony.

And one of them took her thyrsus and struck it on the rock; and from the rock there gushed a spring of limpid water; another struck her wand down into the earth, and there the god made a fountain of wine spring up; and any who wanted milk had only to scratch the earth with the tip of her fingers, and there was the white stream flowing for her to drink; and from the ivy-bound thyrsus a sweet ooze of honey dripped. Oh! if you had been there and seen all this, you would have entreated with prayers this god whom you now accuse.

Well, we herdsmen and shepherds gathered and stood talking together, and arguing about these strange and extraordinary doings. And one fellow, a gadder up to town, and a good speaker, addressed the rest of us. 'You who live on the holy mountain heights,' he said, 'how if we should hunt down the king's mother, Agauë, bring her away from these orgies, and do the king a service?' We thought it was a good suggestion; so we hid ourselves among the leafy bushes and waited our chance.

When the set time came, the women began brandishing their wands and preparing to dance, calling in unison on the son of Zeus, 'Iacchus! Bromius!' And the whole mountain, and the wild beasts too, became a part of their joyful dance – there was nothing that was not roused to leap and run.

Now Agauë as she ran happened to pass close to me; so I sprang out of the ambush where we lay hidden, meaning to capture her.

But she cried out, 'Oh, my swift hounds, we are being hunted by these men. Come, then, and follow; arm yourselves with the thyrsus, and follow me!'

So we fled, and escaped being torn in pieces by these possessed women. But our cattle were feeding there on the fresh grass; and the Bacchae attacked them, with their bare hands. You could see Agauë take up a bellowing young heifer with full udders, and hold it by the legs with her two arms stretched wide. Others were tearing our cows limb from limb, and you could see perhaps some ribs or a cleft hoof being tossed high and low; and pieces of bloody flesh hung dripping on the pine-branches. And bulls, which one moment were savagely looking along their horns, the next were thrown bodily to the ground, dragged down by the soft hands of girls – thousands of them; and they stripped the flesh off their bodies faster than you could wink your royal eyes.

Then, like birds, skimming the ground as they ran, they scoured the plain which stretches by the river Asopus and produces a rich harvest for Thebes; and like an enemy army they bore down on the villages of Hysiae and Erythrae, which lie on the low slopes of Cithaeron, and ransacked them. They snatched up children out of the houses; all the plunder they laid on their shoulders stayed safely there without any fastening; nothing fell to the dark earth, not bronze or iron even; they carried fire on their heads, and their hair was not burnt.

The villagers, of course, were furious at being plundered by the Bacchae, and they resisted with weapons; and then, my lord, was an astonishing sight to behold. The spears cast by the villagers drew no blood; but the women, hurling the thyrsus like a spear, dealt wounds; those women turned the men to flight. There was the power of a god in that.

Then they went back to the place they had started from, to those fountains the god had made flow for them. And they washed off the blood, and the snakes licked the stains clean from their cheeks.

So, master, whoever this god may be, receive him in our city.

He has great power in many ways; but especially, as I hear, it was he who gave men the gift of the vine as a cure for sorrow. And if there were no more wine, why, there's an end of love, and of every other pleasure in life.

CHORUS
I hesitate to speak freely before the king; yet I will say it: there is no greater god than Dionysus.

PENTHEUS
This outrageous Bacchism advances on us like a spreading fire, disgracing us before all Hellas. We must waste no time. [*To the* HERDSMAN] Go at once to the Electran gate; tell all my men who bear shields, heavy or light, all who ride fast horses or twang the bowstring, to meet me there in readiness for an assault on the Bacchae. This is past all bearing, if we are to let women so defy us.

DIONYSUS
You refuse, Pentheus, to listen to what I say or to alter your behaviour. Yet, in spite of all I have suffered at your hands, I warn you to stay where you are and not to take arms against a god. Dionysus will not stand quietly by and see you drive his Bacchae from their mountain rites.

PENTHEUS
I want no instruction from you. You have escaped from your fetters – be content; or I will punish you again.

DIONYSUS
You are a mortal, he is a god. If I were you I would control my rage and sacrifice to him, rather than kick against the pricks.

PENTHEUS
Sacrifice! I will indeed – an offering of women's blood, slaughtered as they deserve in the glens of Cithaeron.

DIONYSUS

You will all be put to flight. It would be disgraceful for the wands of Bacchic women to rout your brazen shields.

PENTHEUS

This foreigner is an impossible man to deal with; in prison or out, he will not hold his tongue.

DIONYSUS

My friend! A happy settlement may still be found.

PENTHEUS

How? By making me a slave to my own slaves?

DIONYSUS

I will bring those women here, without use of weapons.

PENTHEUS

Heaven help us, you are plotting some trick.

DIONYSUS

A trick? If I use my power to save you?

PENTHEUS

This is something you have arranged with the women, so that this orgy may continue.

DIONYSUS

This is something, certainly, that I have arranged – not with them, but with the god.

PENTHEUS

That is enough from you. – Bring out my armour, there!

DIONYSUS [*with an authoritative shout*]
Wait! [*Then, quietly*] Would you like to *see* those women, sitting together, there in the mountains?

PENTHEUS
Yes, indeed; I would give a large sum of gold to see them.

From now on DIONYSUS *gradually establishes a complete ascendancy over* PENTHEUS

DIONYSUS
And what has betrayed you into this great eagerness?

PENTHEUS
I am not eager to see them drunk; that would be a painful sight.

DIONYSUS
Yet you would be glad to see a sight that would pain you?

PENTHEUS
I would, yes; if I could sit quietly under the pine-trees and watch.

DIONYSUS
However secretly you go they will track you down.

PENTHEUS
You are quite right. I will go openly.

DIONYSUS
Shall I show you the way, then? You will venture on this?

PENTHEUS
Lead me there at once; I am impatient.

DIONYSUS
Then, first dress yourself in a fine linen gown.

PENTHEUS
Why a linen gown? Must I change my sex?

DIONYSUS
They will kill you if you are seen there dressed as a man.

PENTHEUS
You are quite right; you think of everything!

DIONYSUS
It was Dionysus who inspired me with that thought.

PENTHEUS
How can your suggestion best be carried out?

DIONYSUS
I will come indoors with you and dress you.

PENTHEUS
Dress me? Not in woman's clothes? I would be ashamed.

DIONYSUS
You have lost your enthusiasm for watching the Maenads.

PENTHEUS
What kind of dress do you say you will put on me?

DIONYSUS
I will cover your head with long, flowing hair.

PENTHEUS
And after that? What will my costume look like?

DIONYSUS
A robe falling to your feet; and a snood on your head.

PENTHEUS
Anything else?

DIONYSUS
A thyrsus in your hand, and a dappled fawnskin round you.

PENTHEUS
I could never wear woman's clothes.

DIONYSUS
If you join battle with the Bacchae there will be bloodshed.

PENTHEUS
You are right; I must first go to spy on them.

DIONYSUS
That is wiser than inviting violence by using it.

PENTHEUS
And how shall I get through the streets of Thebes without being
seen?

DIONYSUS
We will go by lonely ways; I will guide you.

PENTHEUS
I must not be laughed at by the Bacchae – anything rather than
that. Now I will go in, and decide how best to act.

DIONYSUS
You may. My own preparations are all made.

PENTHEUS
I will go, then; and I will either march sword in hand to the
mountain – or else I will follow your advice.   [*Exit* PENTHEUS]

DIONYSUS

Women, this man is walking into the net. He will visit the Bacchae; and there he shall be punished with death.

Dionysus (for you are not far away), all is now in your hands. Let us be revenged on him! And – first assail him with fantastic madness and drive him out of his mind; for while he is sane he will never consent to put on a woman's clothes; but once he has broken from the rein of reason he will put them on. I long to set Thebes laughing at him, as I lead him dressed like a woman through the streets; to humble him from the arrogance with which he threatened me at first.

Now I will go, to array Pentheus in the dress which he will take down with him to the world of the dead, slaughtered by his own mother's hands. And he shall know the son of Zeus, Dionysus; who, though most gentle to mankind, can prove a god of terror irresistible.

DIONYSUS *follows* PENTHEUS *into the palace*

CHORUS

O for long nights of worship, gay
With the pale gleam of dancing feet,
With head tossed high to the dewy air –
Pleasure mysterious and sweet!
O for the joy of a fawn at play
In the fragrant meadow's green delight,
Who has leapt out free from the woven snare,
Away from the terror of chase and flight,
And the huntsman's shout, and the straining pack,
And skims the sand by the river's brim
With the speed of wind in each aching limb,
To the blessed lonely forest where
The soil's unmarked by a human track,
And leaves hang thick and the shades are dim.

What prayer should we call wise?
What gift of heaven should man
Count a more noble prize,
A prayer more prudent, than
To stretch a conquering arm
Over the fallen crest
Of those who wished us harm?
And what is noble every heart loves best.

Slow, yet unfailing, move the Powers
Of heaven with the moving hours.
When mind runs mad, dishonours God,
And worships self and senseless pride,
Then Law eternal wields the rod.
Still heaven hunts down the impious man,
Though divine subtlety may hide
Time's creeping foot. No mortal ought
To challenge Time – to overbear
Custom in act, or age in thought.
All men, at little cost, may share
The blessing of a pious creed;
Truths more than mortal, which began
In the beginning, and belong
To very nature – these indeed
Reign in our world, are fixed and strong.

What prayer should we call wise?
What gift of heaven should man
Count a more noble prize,
A prayer more prudent, than
To stretch a conquering arm
Over the fallen crest
Of those who wished us harm?
And what is noble every heart loves best.

Blest is the man who cheats the stormy sea
And safely moors beside the sheltering quay;
So, blest is he who triumphs over trial.
One man, by various means, in wealth or strength
Outdoes his neighbour; hope in a thousand hearts
Colours a thousand different dreams; at length
Some find a dear fulfilment, some denial.
    But this I say,
    That he who best
    Enjoys each passing day
    Is truly blest.

Enter DIONYSUS. *He turns to call* PENTHEUS

DIONYSUS
Come, perverse man, greedy for sights you should not see, impatient for deeds you should not do – Pentheus! Come out of the palace and show yourself to me, wearing the garb of a frenzied Bacchic woman, ready to spy on your mother and all her company!

Enter PENTHEUS *dressed as a Bacchic devotee. He is dazed, and entirely subservient to* DIONYSUS

Ah! You look exactly like one of Cadmus' daughters.

PENTHEUS
Why – I seem to see two suns; I see a double Thebes, and the city wall with its seven gates – double! I see you leading me forward – you are like a bull, you have horns growing on your head. Tell me, were you an animal a little while ago? You have certainly become a bull.

DIONYSUS
The god did not favour us before; now he is with us, and we have made our peace with him. Now you see as you ought to see.

PENTHEUS

Well, how do I look? Do you think I stand like Ino or like my mother Agauë?

DIONYSUS

I think you are their very image. Wait – this curl of hair is out of place, not as I arranged it under your snood.

PENTHEUS

I must have shaken it loose indoors, tossing my head up and down like a Bacchic worshipper.

DIONYSUS

Come, it is for me to look after you; I will set it straight. Now, lift your head.

PENTHEUS

There, *you* put it right. I depend entirely on you.

DIONYSUS

And your girdle is loose; and the folds of your gown are not hanging straight to your ankles.

PENTHEUS

I agree, they are not – at least, here by the right foot. But on the other side the gown hangs well to the heel.

DIONYSUS

I think you will reckon me the chief of your friends, when you see the Bacchae and find to your surprise how well they are behaving – will you not?

But PENTHEUS is not listening

PENTHEUS

Ought I to hold my thyrsus in this hand or in the right, to look more like a Bacchanal?

DIONYSUS

Hold it in your right hand, and raise it at the same time as you raise your right foot. [PENTHEUS *attempts it*] I am glad you are so – changed in mind.

PENTHEUS

Do you think I could lift up on my shoulders the glens of Cithaeron, with all the women dancing there?

DIONYSUS

You could, if you wished. Before, your mind was diseased; now, it is as it should be.

PENTHEUS

Shall we take crowbars? Or shall I simply set my shoulder, or my arm, against the mountain peaks, and tear them up with my hands?

DIONYSUS

No, you must not destroy the homes of the Nymphs, and the haunts where Pan sits piping.

PENTHEUS

You are right. Women are not to be subdued by brute force. I will hide among the pine-trees.

DIONYSUS

Hide? Yes! You shall find the right hiding-place to hide you – coming like a crafty spy to watch the Maenads!

PENTHEUS

Yes, I can picture them – like birds in the thickets, wrapped in the sweet snare of love.

DIONYSUS

That is the very thing you are going to look for; and perhaps you will catch them – if you are not first caught yourself.

PENTHEUS
Now lead me through the central streets of Thebes. There is no one dares to do this – I am the only *man* among them.

DIONYSUS
You alone suffer for the whole city – you alone; and the struggle that awaits you is your destined ordeal. Come; I will see you safely there; another shall bring you home.

PENTHEUS
You mean my mother?

DIONYSUS
A sight for all to see.

PENTHEUS
It is for that I am going.

DIONYSUS
You will be carried home –

PENTHEUS
What splendour that will be!

DIONYSUS
– in your mother's arms.

PENTHEUS
Why, you make a weakling of me!

DIONYSUS
That is – one way of putting it.

PENTHEUS
Yet it is what I deserve. [*Exit* PENTHEUS]

DIONYSUS

Pentheus, you are a man to make men fear; and fearful will be
your end – an end that shall raise your fame to the height of
heaven. Stretch out your hands, Agauë, and you her sisters,
daughters of Cadmus! I am bringing the young man to his battle;
and I and Dionysus shall be victors. [*Then he adds quietly*] What
more shall happen, the event will show.

Exit DIONYSUS

CHORUS

     Hounds of Madness, fly to the mountain, fly
     Where Cadmus' daughters are dancing in ecstasy!
     Madden them like a frenzied herd stampeding,
     Against the madman hiding in woman's clothes
     To spy on the Maenads' rapture!
     First his mother shall see him craning his neck
     Down from a rounded rock or a withered trunk,
     And shout to the Maenads, 'Who is the man, you Bacchae,
     Who has come to the mountain, come to the mountain spying
     On the swift wild mountain-dances of Cadmus' daughters?
     Which of you is his mother?
     No, that lad never lay in a woman's womb;
     A lioness gave him suck, or a Libyan Gorgon!'

     Justice, now be revealed! Now let your sword
     Thrust – through and through – to sever the throat
     Of the godless, lawless, shameless son of Echion,
     Who sprang from the womb of Earth!

     See! With contempt of right, with a reckless rage
     To combat your and your mother's mysteries, Bacchus,
     With maniac fury out he goes, stark mad,
     For a trial of strength against *your* invincible arm!
     The sober and humble heart
     That accords the gods their due without carp or cavil,

And knows that his days are as dust, shall live untouched.
I have no wish to grudge the wise their wisdom;
But the joys *I* seek are greater, outshine all others,
And lead our life to goodness and loveliness:
The joy of the holy heart
That night and day is bent to honour the gods
And disown all custom that breaks the bounds of right.

Justice, now be revealed! Now let your sword
Thrust – through and through – to sever the throat
Of the godless, lawless, shameless son of Echion,
Who sprang from the womb of Earth!

Then with growing excitement, shouting in unison, and
dancing to the rhythm of their words

> Come, Dionysus!
> Come, and appear to us!
> Come like a bull or a
> Hundred-headed serpent,
> Come like a lion snorting
> Flame from your nostrils!
> Swoop down, Bacchus, on the
> Hunter of the Bacchae;
> Smile at him and snare him;
> Then let the stampeding
> Herd of the Maenads
> Throw him and throttle him,
> Catch, trip, trample him to death!

Enter a MESSENGER

MESSENGER

O house once glorious throughout Hellas, house of the old Sidonian
king who sowed in this soil the dragon's earth-born crop! How I
weep for you! I am a slave; but a good slave feels the blow that
strikes his master.

CHORUS

What has happened? Have you news from the mountains?

MESSENGER

Pentheus, the son of Echion, is dead.

CHORUS

Dionysus, god of rapture! Your power is revealed!

MESSENGER

What? What did you say? Do you even exult at the cruel end that has overtaken my master?

CHORUS

I am no Greek; I sing for joy in a foreign tune. Now I've no need to cower in terror of prison.

MESSENGER

Do you suppose Thebes has no men left to take command?

CHORUS

Dionysus commands *me*; not Thebes, but Dionysus.

MESSENGER

Allowance must be made for you; yet, when irreparable wrong has been done, it is shameful to rejoice.

CHORUS

Tell me what happened; tell me, how did he die – this tyrant pursuing his tyranny?

MESSENGER

When we had left the houses of Thebes behind, and crossed the river Asopus, we began climbing the foothills of Cithaeron,

Pentheus and I – I was attending my master – and that foreigner who was showing us the way to what we were to see.

Well, first we sat down in a grassy glade; we kept our footsteps and our talk as quiet as possible, so as to see without being seen. We were in a valley full of streams, with cliffs on either side; and there, under the close shade of pine-trees, the Maenads were sitting, their hands busy at their happy tasks. Some of them were twining with fresh leaves a thyrsus that had lost its ivy; others, like foals let loose from the painted yokes, were singing holy songs to each other in turn.

But the ill-fated Pentheus did not see these women; and he said, 'From where we are standing, my friend, I cannot clearly make out these pretended worshippers, these Maenads; if I climbed a towering pine-tree on the cliff-side I could have a proper view of their shameful behaviour.'

And then – I saw that foreigner do an amazing thing. He took hold of the topmost skiey branch of a pine and dragged it down, down, down to the dark earth. It was bent in a circle as a bow is bent, as the curve of a wheel, drawn with peg and line, bends the running rim to its own shape; so the foreigner took that mountain-pine in his hands and bent it to the ground – a thing no mortal man could do. Then he set Pentheus on the top branches, and began letting the tree spring upright, slipping it steadily through his grip, and taking care not to unseat him; and the pine-trunk straightened itself and soared into the soaring sky with the King sitting astride; so that he was more plainly visible to the women than they were to him.

And he was just coming into view on his lofty perch – the foreigner was nowhere to be seen – when a voice – I suppose it was Dionysus – pealed out from heaven: 'Women! I bring you the man who made a mockery of you, and of me, and of my holy rites. Now punish him.' And in the very moment the voice spoke, a flash of unearthly fire stretched between the sky and the ground.

The whole air fell silent. The wooded glade held every leaf silent. You could hear no cry of any beast. The women had not caught distinctly what the voice said; they stood up and gazed around. Then came a second word of command. As soon as Cadmus' daughters recognized the clear bidding of Bacchus, they darted forward with the speed of doves on the wing, and all the Bacchae after them. Up the valley, along by the stream, over the rocks they went leaping on, possessed with the very breath of the god. When they saw the King sitting in the tree, first they climbed the cliff where it rose up like a battlement, and with all their strength pelted him with pieces of rock, or aimed pine-branches at him like javelins. Some were hurling the thyrsus at their pitiable target; but the shots fell short – the height was too great for all their efforts; while the wretched man sat there trapped and helpless.

At last, with a force like lightning, they tore down branches of oak, and used these as levers, trying to tear out the tree's roots. All their struggles were useless. Then Agauë spoke to them: 'Come, you Maenads, stand round the tree and grip it. We must catch this climbing beast, or he will reveal the secret dances of Dionysus.' A thousand hands grasped the tree; and they tore it from the earth. Then from his high perch plunging and crashing to the ground came Pentheus, with one incessant scream as he understood what end was near.

First his mother, as priestess, began the ritual of death, and fell upon him. He tore off the headband from his hair, that his wretched mother might recognize him and not kill him. 'Mother!' he cried, touching her cheek, 'it is I, your son, Pentheus, whom you bore to Echion. O Mother, have mercy on me; I have sinned, but I am your son: do not kill me!'

Agauë was foaming at the mouth, her eyes were rolling wildly. She was not in her right mind; she was under the power of Dionysus; and she would not listen to him. She gripped his right arm between wrist and elbow; she set her foot against his ribs; and she tore his arm off by the shoulder. It was no strength of hers that did it; the god was in her fingers and made it easy. Ino was at him on the other side, tearing at his flesh; and now Autonoë joined them, and the whole pack of raving women. There was a single continuous

yell – Pentheus shrieking as long as life was left in him, the
women howling in triumph. One of them was carrying an arm,
another had a foot with the shoe still on it; the ribs were stripped –
clawed clean. Every hand was thick red with blood; and they were
tossing and catching, to and fro, like a ball, the flesh of Pentheus.

His body lies scattered, some under hard rocks, some in the
deep green woods; it will not be easy to find. His poor head – his
mother is holding it; she has fixed it on the point of her thyrsus,
and carries it openly over the mountain-side, leaving her sisters
dancing with the Maenads. And she is coming here to the palace,
exulting in her fearful and horrible prey, shouting to Bacchus as
her fellow-hunter, calling him her partner in the kill, her comrade
in victory. But Bacchus gives her tears for her reward.

I am going; I want to be far away from this horror before Agauë
comes.

The noblest thing a man can have is a humble and quiet heart
that reveres the gods. I think that is also the wisest thing for a man
to possess, if he will but use it.

Exit

CHORUS
 Let us dance a dance to Bacchus, shout and sing
 For the fall of Pentheus, heir of the dragon's seed,
 Who hid his beard in a woman's gown,
 And sealed his death with the holy sign
 Of ivy wreathing a fennel-reed,
 When bull led man to the ritual slaughter-ring.
 Frenzied daughters of Cadmus, what renown
 Your victory wins you – such a song
 As groans must stifle, tears must drown!
 Emblem of conquest, brave and fine! –
 A mother's hand, defiled
 With blood and dripping red
 Caresses the torn head
 Of her own murdered child!

But look! I see Pentheus' mother, Agauë, running towards the palace, with eyes wildly rolling. Welcome the worshipping company of Dionysus!

AGAUË *appears, frenzied and panting, with* PENTHEUS' *head held in her hand. The rest of her band of devotees, whom the* CHORUS *saw approaching with her, do not enter; but a few are seen standing by the entrance, where they wait until the end of the play.*

AGAUË
Women of Asia! Worshippers of Bacchus!

AGAUË *tries to show them* PENTHEUS' *head; they shrink from it*

CHORUS   Why do you urge me? Oh!

AGAUË   I am bringing home from the mountains
                A vine-branch freshly cut,
                For the gods have blessed our hunting.

CHORUS   We see it . . . and welcome you in fellowship.

AGAUË   I caught him without a trap,
                A lion-cub, young and wild.
                Look, you may see him: there!

CHORUS   Where was it?

AGAUË   On Cithaeron;
                The wild and empty mountain –

CHORUS   Cithaeron!

AGAUË   . . . spilt his life-blood.

CHORUS   Who shot him?

AGAUË   I was first;
              All the women are singing,
              'Honour to great Agauë!'

CHORUS   And then – who next?

AGAUË   Why, Cadmus' . . .

CHORUS   What – Cadmus?

AGAUË   Yes, his daughters –
              But after me, after me –
              Laid their hands to the kill.
              To-day was a splendid hunt!
              Come now, join in the feast!

CHORUS   What, wretched woman? *Feast?*

AGAUË [*tenderly stroking the head as she holds it*]
              This calf is young: how thickly
              The new-grown hair goes crisping
              Up to his delicate crest!

CHORUS   Indeed, his long hair makes him
              Look like some wild creature.

AGAUË   The god is a skilled hunter;
              And he poised his hunting women,
              And hurled them at the quarry.

CHORUS   True, our god is a hunter.

AGAUË   Do you praise me?

CHORUS   Yes, we praise you.

AGAUË   So will the sons of Cadmus . . .

CHORUS   And Pentheus too, Agauë?

AGAUË   Yes, he will praise his mother
                For the lion-cub she killed.

CHORUS   Oh, fearful!

AGAUË   Ay, fearful!

CHORUS   You are happy?

AGAUË   I am enraptured;
                Great in the eyes of the world,
                Great are the deeds I've done,
                And the hunt that I hunted there!

CHORUS
Then, poor Agauë, show this triumphant spoil of yours that you've
carried home – show it to the people of Thebes.

AGAUË
Come, then, all you Thebans who live in this lofty and lovely city,
come and see the beast we have caught and killed – we, Cadmus'
daughters; caught not with nets or thonged Thessalian javelins,
but with our own white arms and fingers. After this, should huntsmen boast, who buy their paltry tools from the armourer? We with
our bare hands caught this quarry, then tore it limb from limb.

   Where is my father? Let him come here! And my son Pentheus,
where is he? Let him get a strong ladder, and take this head, and
climb up and nail it to the top of the palace wall, this lion that I
hunted and brought home!

Enter CADMUS *with attendants bearing the body of* PENTHEUS

CADMUS
Come, men. Bring your sad burden that was Pentheus; bring him
to his home. I found the fragments of his body scattered in a
thousand places, no two together, about the glens of Cithaeron, or
hidden in thick woods; and with weary search I gathered them,
and have brought them here.

I had already returned with old Teiresias from the Bacchic
dance, and was inside the walls of the city, when news was brought
me of my daughters' terrible deed. I turned straight back to the
mountain; and here I bring my son, killed by the Maenads. I saw
Autonoë, who bore Actaeon to Aristaeus, and her sister Ino, there
among the copses, still in their unhappy frenzy; but I understand
that Agauë came raving towards the palace – it is true, there she
is! Oh, what a terrible sight!

AGAUË
Father! You may boast as loudly as you will, that no man living
is so blest in his daughters; I mean all three, but myself especially.
I have left weaving at the loom for greater things – for hunting
wild beasts with my bare hands. See here what I carry in my arms;
this is the prize I won; I have brought it to hang on your palace
wall. Take it, Father; hold it. Be proud of my hunting, and call
your friends to a banquet; let them all envy and congratulate you,
for the splendour of my deed.

CADMUS
O anguish unmeasured, intolerable! O pitiful hands – your splendid deed is murder! What victim is this you would lay at the gods'
feet, calling Thebes, and me, to a banquet? Your suffering is worst,
but mine is next. Dionysus, god of joy, has been just, but too cruel.
He was born of my blood, and he has destroyed my house.

AGAUË

How ill-humoured old age makes a man! How he scowls at me! I wish that my son were a great hunter, like his mother, pursuing wild beasts with all the young men of Thebes; but he can only fight against gods. Father, you must reason with him. Let someone call him here before me, to see my good fortune.

CADMUS

Oh, my daughters! If you come to understand what you have done, how terrible your suffering will be! But if you remain always as you are now, though you could not be called happy, at least you will not know your own misery.

AGAUË

Misery? What is wrong? Where is my cause for misery?

CADMUS

First, turn your eyes this way – look at the sky.

AGAUË

I am looking. Why do you tell me to look at it?

CADMUS

Is it still the same, or does it seem to you to have changed?

AGAUË

It is brighter than before – more luminous.

CADMUS

And this madness you suffered from – is it still with you?

AGAUË

I do not know what you mean. But I feel a change in my mind; my thoughts are somehow clearer.

CADMUS
Can you now hear and answer clearly?

AGAUË
Yes . . . I have forgotten what we said just now, Father.

CADMUS
When you were married, whose house did you come to?

AGAUË
You gave me to Echion, who was said to have been sown in the
ground.

CADMUS
Then, Echion had a son born to him – who was he?

AGAUË
Pentheus – my son and his father's.

CADMUS
Yes: and whose head is that you hold in your arms?

AGAUË
A lion's – or so the women said who hunted it.

CADMUS
Now look straight at it; it is not much trouble to look.

AGAUË *looks at the head in silence; then cries out*

AGAUË
Oh! What am I looking at? What am I holding?

CADMUS
Look at it steadily, and understand more clearly.

AGAUË

I see – O gods, what horror! What torture!

CADMUS

Does this seem to you like a lion?

AGAUË

No, it is Pentheus' head I hold in my accursed hand.

CADMUS

Tears have been shed for him already – before you knew it was he.

AGAUË

Who killed him? How did he come into my hands?

CADMUS

O bitter truth, revealed in a cruel hour!

AGAUË

Tell me – my heart is bursting – I must know the rest.

CADMUS

You killed him – you and your sisters.

AGAUË

Where was it done? At home? Or where else?

CADMUS

Where Actaeon was torn by hounds.

AGAUË

Cithaeron? What evil fate brought Pentheus there?

CADMUS

He went in scorn of Dionysus and your frenzied worship.

AGAUË

But how was it we were all there?

CADMUS

You were mad; the whole city was possessed by Dionysus.

AGAUË

Now I understand: Dionysus has destroyed us.

CADMUS

He was insulted and abused. You did not acknowledge his god-head.

AGAUË

Where is the dear body of my son, Father?

CADMUS

It is here. I searched long for it, and brought it.

AGAUË

Is it decently composed, limb to limb?

CADMUS

Not yet; we came here as quickly as possible.

AGAUË

I will do it myself, if I may be allowed to touch him.

CADMUS

You will be allowed; your guilt is not greater than his.

AGAUË

But what part had Pentheus in my madness?

CADMUS

He was like you in not reverencing Dionysus. Therefore the god has joined all in one destruction, you and your sisters, and Pentheus, to strike down my house and me. I have no son; and now I see the child of your womb, my unhappy daughter, cut off by a shameful and horrible death. Pentheus, dear boy, my daughter's child, this house looked to you as its head; you were its bond of strength; and Thebes feared you. No man would slight your old grandfather if he saw you near; you would give him his deserts. Now I, Cadmus the Great, who sowed in the ground the seed of the Theban race, and reaped a glorious harvest, shall live, a dishonoured exile, far from my home.

O dearest son – yes, even in death you shall be held most dear to me – never again will you touch my beard, and call me Grandfather, and put your arm round me and say, 'Who has wronged you, or insulted you? Who is unkind to you or vexes you? Tell me, Grandfather, that I may punish him.' . . . Never again. Now there is only misery for me, suffering for you, tears for your mother, torment for all our family.

If there be any man who derides the unseen world, let him consider the death of Pentheus, and acknowledge the gods.

CHORUS
Cadmus, I grieve for you. Your grandson suffered justly, but you most cruelly.

AGAUË
Father, you see how one terrible hour has shattered my whole life, and turned my pride to shame, my happiness to horror. Now I long only to compose my son's body for burial, and lament for him; and then to go away and die. But I do not know if this is lawful; my hands are filthy with a pollution of their own making. When I have spilt the blood that is my own, torn the flesh that grew in my own womb, how can I, without offence to the gods, clasp him to my breast, or chant his ritual dirge? Yet I beg you, if you think it not blasphemous, let me touch my son, and say farewell to that dear body which I loved, and destroyed unknowing. It

is right that you should pity, for you suffer too, although you have not sinned.

CADMUS

My daughter, you and I and our whole house are crushed and broken by the anger of Dionysus. It is not for me to keep you from your son. Only I would warn you to steel your heart against a sight that must be fearful to any eyes, but most of all to a mother's. [*To his attendants*] Lay your burden here before her, and remove the covering, that Agaue may see her son.

The coffin is laid on the ground before AGAUE
who kneels beside it

AGAUE

O dearest child, how unnatural are these tears, that should have fallen from your eyes upon my dead face. Now I shall die with none to weep for me. I am justly punished; for in pride I blasphemed the god Dionysus, and did not understand the things I ought to have understood. You too are punished for the same sin; and I cannot tell whether your fate or mine is the more terrible. But since you have suffered with me, you will forgive me both for what I did, not knowing what I did, and for what I do now, touching you with unholy hands – at once your cruellest enemy and your dearest lover.

Now I place your limbs as they should lie; I kiss the flesh that my own body fed, my own care reared to manhood. Come, Father, help me; lay his poor head here; as far as we can, make all exact and seemly.

O dearest face, O young fresh cheek; O kingly eyes, your light now darkened! O my son! See, with this veil I now cover your head, your torn and bloodstained limbs.

Now take him up and carry him to burial – a king lured to a shameful death by the anger of a god.

DIONYSUS *appears above the wall of the palace*

CHORUS

But look! What is this? It is he, our lord Dionysus himself, no
longer disguised as mortal, but in the glory of his godhead!

DIONYSUS

Behold me, a god great and powerful, Dionysus, immortal son of
Zeus and Semele!

I come to the City of Seven Gates, to Thebes, whose men and
women mocked me, denied my divinity, and refused to receive my
holy rites. Now they see clearly the result of impious folly. The
royal house is overthrown; the city's streets are full of guilty fear,
as every Theban repents too late for his blindness and blasphemy.
First and chief in sin was this man Pentheus, who not only rejected
my just claims, but put me in fetters and insulted me. Therefore
death came to him in the most shameful way of all, at the hands of
his own mother. This fate he has justly suffered; for no god can see
his worship scorned, and hear his name profaned, and not pursue
vengeance to the utmost limit; that mortal men may know that the
gods are greater than they.

Now listen further, while I reveal what is destined for the people
of Thebes. The day will come when they will be driven from their
city to wander East and West over the earth; for Zeus will not
suffer a godless city to remain.

Agauë and her sisters must leave Thebes this very day; their
exile will prove a full and just penance for the foul pollution they
have incurred in this bloodshed. Never again shall they see their
native land; for it is an offence to piety that hands so defiled
should remain to take part in the city's sacrifices.

Now, Cadmus, I will tell you what suffering you yourself are
destined to fulfil. You shall change your form to a serpent; and
your wife Harmonia, whom you, though mortal, received from her
divine father Ares, shall likewise change to a beast of the earth,
and become a snake. Thus says the oracle of Zeus: You, at the

head of a barbaric army, shall with your wife drive a pair of oxen
yoked to a wagon; with your innumerable host you shall destroy
many cities; but when they plunder the temple of Apollo's oracle,
their reward shall be sorrow at their home-coming. But you yourself and Harmonia shall be saved by Ares, who shall bestow on
you immortal life among the blessed ones.

I, who tell you this, am Dionysus, son of no mortal father, but
of Zeus. If you all had chosen wisdom, when you would not, you
would have found the son of Zeus your friend, and you would now
be happy.

CADMUS
Dionysus, have mercy on us; we have sinned.

DIONYSUS
You recognize me too late; when you should have known me, you
did not.

CADMUS
All this we have realized; but your vengeance is too heavy.

DIONYSUS
I am a god; and you insulted me.

CADMUS
Gods should not be like men, keeping anger for ever.

DIONYSUS
Zeus my father ordained this from the beginning.

AGAUË
All hope is gone, Father. Our sentence is passed: we are exiles.

DIONYSUS
Why then put off what is inevitable? [*Exit* DIONYSUS]

CADMUS

O my daughter, what utter misery and horror has overtaken us all – you, and your sisters, and me your unhappy father. In my old age I must leave my home and travel to strange lands. Further than that, it is foretold that I shall lead a mixed barbarian horde against Hellas. Both I and my wife, Harmonia, child of Ares, must take the brute form of serpents, and thus I am to lead her, at the head of an armed force, to desecrate the altars and tombs of the Hellenes. And I am to find no respite from suffering; I may not even cross the deep-flowing stream of Acheron to find peace in death.

AGAUË

And I shall live in exile, separated from you, Father.

CADMUS

Poor child! Why do you throw your arms round me, cherishing my white hair as a swan cares for its old and helpless ones?

AGAUË

Where am I to turn, driven from my home and country?

CADMUS

I do not know, child; your father is little help to you.

AGAUË

    Farewell, my home; farewell the land I know.
    Exiled, accursed and wretched, now I go
    Forth from this door where first I came a bride.

CADMUS

    Go, daughter; find some secret place to hide
    Your shame and sorrow.

AGAUË   Father, I weep for you.

CADMUS
> I for your suffering, and your sisters' too.

AGAUË
> There is strange tyranny in the god who sent
> Against your house this cruel punishment.

CADMUS
> Not strange: our citizens despised his claim,
> And you, and they, put him to open shame.

AGAUË
> Father, farewell.

CADMUS   Poor child! I cannot tell
> How you can *fare well*; yet I say, Farewell.

AGAUË
> I go to lead my sisters by the hand
> To share my wretchedness in a foreign land.

*She turns to the Theban women who have been waiting at the edge
of the stage*

> Come, see me forth.
>   Gods, lead me to some place
> Where loath'd Cithaeron may not see my face,
> Nor I Cithaeron. I have had my fill
> Of mountain-ecstasy; now take who will
> My holy ivy-wreath, my thyrsus-rod,
> All that reminds me how I served this god!

Exit, followed by CADMUS

CHORUS

Gods manifest themselves in many forms,
Bring many matters to surprising ends;
The things we thought would happen do not happen;
The unexpected God makes possible:
And that is what has happened here to-day.

Exeunt

NOTES

MEDEA

3 *The Argo:* Jason was the son of Aeson, half-brother of Pelias king of Iolcus in Thessaly. To get rid of Jason, who was a rival for his throne, Pelias persuaded him to go to Colchis, at the eastern end of the Black Sea, and fetch the Golden Fleece. Jason sailed to Colchis in the ship called *Argo*, and accomplished his task with the help of Medea, daughter of the king of Colchis. Medea drugged the dragon which guarded the treasure; and Jason promised to marry her. They escaped, and Medea's brother came with them. When the king pursued them, Medea killed her brother, cut him in pieces, and threw him into the sea, so that the king might be delayed by the necessity of re-covering his son's body. They eventually reached Iolcus. Here Medea contrived the murder of Pelias in the hope that Jason would succeed him; but the people of Iolcus were indignant and expelled Jason and Medea, who subsequently settled in Corinth.

19 *The fire-breathing bulls:* The king of Colchis had required this task of Jason, in return for his permission to seek the Golden Fleece.

By his own daughters' hands: Medea persuaded the daughters of Pelias that they could renew their father's youth by killing him and boiling his flesh.

32 *I'll anoint my gifts:* When does Medea do this? The action of the play gives her no opportunity. The dress is brought in a casket, and she sends it off without looking at it.

48 *The blue Symplegades:* The 'Clashing Rocks' (already referred to in line 2), near the mouth of the Bosporus, the gateway to the Black Sea.

51 *Battering at these doors:* The Greek apparently means 'battering at these doors and unbarring them'. But the bars were certainly on the inside, and Jason was calling for someone else to move them. The word could also mean 'prizing them open with levers'; but this involves further difficulties. So in the translation the second verb is omitted.

HIPPOLYTUS

59 *The Cyprian:* The Greek name 'Aphrodite' is native to Homeric verse and fits awkwardly into iambics; so that 'Kupris', 'The Cyprian', is almost everywhere used in tragedy. (This name, in fact, frequently drops its personal meaning and becomes an abstract noun for 'sexual love'.) In the translation I have kept 'Aphrodite' throughout for the sake of clarity.

The Amazon: the Queen of the Amazons, Hippolyta, captured in war by Theseus. Shakespeare in *A Midsummer Night's Dream* makes her Theseus' honoured bride; but in the original legend she was a virgin queen subdued by force to the bed of her conqueror. Euripides plainly has this less happy situation in mind as the psychological background of the character of Hippolytus.

63 *To me she is nothing at all!:* The Greek phrase is an ironically polite dismissal, 'Many good-byes to her!' This blasphemy is unconsciously echoed by Theseus on p. 98, in reference to divination by means of birds. As there seems to be no suitable ironic phrase in English to fit both passages, I have used a plain and flat statement.

72 *O my mother!:* Phaedra was the daughter of Pasiphaë, who conceived an unnatural passion for a bull, and subsequently gave birth to the monster called the Minotaur. For this sense of hereditary guilt compare Theseus' words on p. 91, 'Far from here this harvest grew', etc.

74 *The Queen's pitiful cry:* This may refer to Phaedra's words, 'It is he, the Amazon's son!' But presumably during the Nurse's speech Phaedra would be audibly weeping.

75 *And life offers us many pleasures:* Here follow four lines which I have ventured to omit. Their meaning is as follows: '. . . many pleasures: long gossipings and idleness, a pleasant evil; and the sense of shame. Now there are two qualities called "sense of shame"; the one is not evil [i.e. probably, conscience, which

180

deters men from evil]; the other is a curse to families [i.e. shameful deeds]. If these two different qualities were clearly and aptly named, they would not be represented by the same letters.'

There are several passages in other plays where Euripides refers to 'gossip' as a thing likely to corrupt women (e.g. Andromache in *The Women of Troy*). There are also passages where he makes a character discuss the meaning of some word. Both kinds of passage were noted as characteristic of him, and no doubt often parodied. Here, in the middle of Phaedra's agonized confession, such banal irrelevance seems to me to go beyond anything found elsewhere in Euripides, and I therefore regard these lines as possibly or probably spurious.

79 *Of your saying any word about me:* The question how far Phaedra understands the Nurse, whether she tries to deceive herself or remains innocent in intention, is purposely left ambiguous by Euripides, who thus achieves an effect far more dramatic than that of a clear decision either way.

Love, the child of Zeus: Eros.

81 *You are beside the door:* The door is, of course, at the back of the stage; the Chorus are in the *Orchestra*, below and in front of the stage.

89 *A solemn mission of piety:* Theseus has been enquiring formally from an oracle (probably that of Delphi) whether his expiation is now complete (see p. 60, 'His hands stained with the blood of the Pallantides'), and has, ironically enough, returned assured of the favour of Heaven.

90 *That is all I know, Theseus:* It was a dramatic convention that the Chorus must keep secrets entrusted to them. For them to tell at this point all that they know would be to prevent the tragedy. They are provided with an excuse for their silence by Phaedra's solemn charge to them before her last exit. Their failure to save Hippolytus by telling Theseus the truth has often been quoted as an instance of Euripides' failure to reconcile his matter with his medium. But in actual production no difficulty is felt here,

because it is plain to the audience that the Chorus are partly outside the action of the plot. Besides, if Hippolytus will not break his oath, why should the Troezenian women?

95 *Take Orpheus for your lord and prophet:* There seems to be no evidence for any connexion between Hippolytus and Orphism; neither does Hippolytus' remark on p. 63 ('A loaded table's a cheerful sight after hunting'), nor indeed his occupation as a hunter, suggest that he was a vegetarian. Rather Euripides presents Theseus as a middle-aged man who is ready enough to regard fancy cults as responsible for lack of principle in the younger generation—by no means an out-of-date characteristic of middle-aged man.

98 *To me they are nothing at all!:* See p. 63, note.

99 *My unhappy mother!:* The fact that it is this remark which rouses Theseus to a climax of fury gives another strong hint of the tangled emotional relationship implied by Euripides as existing between Theseus and his son. Euripides is following his usual practice of making heroic characters think and feel like fifth-century Athenians. It is noticeable that Theseus realizes he has lost control, quickly recovers himself, and goes out on a rather lame threat.

103 *You have proved a true father to me:* This is the second time (see p. 93) that Theseus has claimed Poseidon for his father; but Artemis twice (pp. 106 and 112) reminds him firmly that his father was the mortal Aegeus, though in her second speech she refers to the giver of the three curses as 'your father'.

107 *I never would have submitted to such dishonour:* The impregnable callousness of this and other remarks of Artemis (especially 'My own hand shall strike down', etc., p. 111) convey Euripides' emphatic valuation of the comforts of religion. Man in extremity must look to himself alone.

113 *When was man more noble?:* It is generally supposed that these words carried a reference to Pericles, who died the year before this play was produced.

THE BACCHAE

118 *Thyrsus:* A light stick of reed or fennel, with fresh strands of ivy twined round it. It was carried by every devotee of Dionysus; and the action of the play illustrates the supernatural power that was held to reside in it.

121 *The celebrant:* Dionysus and the Chorus comprise the typical group of Bacchic worshippers, a male leader with a devoted band of women and girls. The leader *flings himself on the ground* in the climax of ecstasy, when the power of the god enters into him and he becomes possessed.

126 *The ancient word for a* pledge: The translation necessarily expands the original. *Homeros* means 'pledge', and *meros* 'thigh'.

131 *Untie his hands:* The text is uncertain. A very slight alteration gives a completely different meaning: 'You are more mad than he is'– addressed to the guard and his fellows.

141 *The god who makes . . . :* This is conjecturally supplied in place of a missing line.

159 *Were singing holy songs:* The Greek word is *Bacchic* songs. In English this adjective is too often associated with the 'profane' drinking of wine, whereas in this play it always has a religious or at least a ritualistic meaning. In translation I have been deliberately inconsistent, using both *Bacchic* and *holy* for the sake of keeping both ideas operative.

As the curve of a wheel . . . : A difficult passage, of which no satisfactory translation can be made. An amended text gives: 'As a bow by which an untrue wheel, chiselled on a lathe, is swiftly rotated.'

164 *And Pentheus too, Agauë?:* The Chorus are physically shocked by the sight of Agauë and her prey; but their attitude does not change to pity. Agauë has been (in their view, justly) punished

183

for her blasphemy against Dionysus, by being tricked into per-
forming the Bacchic rite of slaughter, not upon the usual
victim, a beast, but upon a man, and that her own son. She is
now an abhorred and polluted creature, unfit for the company
of the 'pure' Bacchae. Hence, though they welcome the punishment of Pentheus, their tone towards Agauë is one not of
admiration but of contempt. This line in particular indicates
the complete absence of pity.

Great in the eyes of the world: Another hint of the 'manifesta-
tion' of the nature of the god.

169 *Not yet; we came here . . . :* This and the following two lines are
missing in the text, and here conjecturally supplied.

170 *. . . and acknowledge the gods:* The climax of the play's irony.

. . . has shattered my whole life: After these words there is a long
gap in the MS. From quotations found in ancient writers editors
have collected a considerable number of fragments probably
belonging to this gap; and the lines here printed are pieced
together from these, in a form something like that we may
expect Euripides to have used. The MS. text begins again with
the words, *You shall change your form to a serpent,* on p. 172.

The puzzling prophecy that follows thereafter raises too
many questions to be dealt with here; there is an excellent note
on this passage in Professor Dodds's edition of the Greek text.